God's Hand in History
During World War II

USS Arizona

VICTOR PENROSA

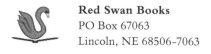

Red Swan Books
PO Box 67063
Lincoln, NE 68506-7063

ISBN: 978-0-994385-1-2 (sc)
ISBN: 978-09974385-2-9 (e)

Library of Congress Control Number: 2017915412

Editors Sandy Kolb and Ellen Mercill
Cover Design and Arizona Illustration by Terrill Birth
On the cover: Painting of Doolittle Raid April 18, 1942
Publisher Victor Penrosa

Rev. date: 9/11/2017

Red Swan Book
PO Box 67063
Lincoln, NE 68506-7063
redswanbooks@gmail.com
www.redswanbooks.com

Contents

Introduction

On July 7, 1937, after a long period of extensive planning to conquer China, Japan started its conquest with what has been called the first battle of World War II. World War II was, without a doubt, the most destructive war the world has ever seen. The number of lives lost varies somewhere between forty million to seventy-five million depending on when historians say the war started. Some say July 7, 1937, was the start. Others state that September 1, 1939, when Germany invaded Poland, or in 1931 when Japan invaded Manchuria. Regardless of the actual date, no one can argue that this war cost more lives and money than any other war in history.

World War II was fought on most continents in the world. Along with the immense loss of life, entire cities and towns were destroyed, and both sides suffered major economic destruction. Germany was turned to rubble, and Great Britain was virtually bankrupt. The European economy had collapsed with only 30 percent of its infrastructure intact, and Japan's was completely destroyed. In addition, much of China, the Philippines, and many Pacific island nations were devastated. The final cost of World War II ended up being $1.6 trillion in 1945, which would approximate $11.2 trillion in 2005. So where was God in all of this?

I would like to make one thing clear; God never intended for us to have wars. He intended we should live in peace and safety forever. According to the Bible, in the book of Genesis, God created man in His own image. ("Man" in the Bible refers to both men and women). God put man in the garden of Eden, a place to live freely in peace. One-day man fell to the temptation of Satan. Because of that, the world has suffered one problem after another.

Mankind's sin established Satan's dominion over the entire earth. In response, God could have destroyed man and started over, but this would have made Him a tyrant. If so, it would prove Satan right, that if you disobeyed, God would wipe you out. So God chose to allow things to move forward even though He was not happy with the choice man made. Yet, from time to time, He has intervened to prevent destruction of this planet.

Some time ago, I was giving a Bible study to a woman. I told her that God was good and was looking out for us. She became very upset and asked me, "If God is so good and caring, then where was He in World War II? Why did millions of people die and so many countries were laid to waste?" She had a very good point. Where was God in all of this? We see that the hand of God was involved, when we hear how individuals survived against all odds. Yet, did God get involved on a much greater scale, such as major battles during the wars? This began to bother me.

Being a student of history, I began looking at World War II. In the D-Day invasion on June 6, 1944, there was only one day that the weather cleared. General Eisenhower, the Allied supreme commander, took a chance to invade France. This took the Germans by surprise. They did not think the Allies would invade with only one day of clear weather, when the forecast called for two weeks of bad weather. Here I first saw how God stepped in and provided an opportunity to change how things could go.

If God changed the weather on D-Day, perhaps He changed it during other battles? I used this as my way to search for how God worked in our lives and in man's wars. I did find more changes in the weather that turned the tide of battle. As I studied, I began to see how God not only used the weather, but He also worked in more subtle ways, such as changing the minds of men. For example, generals did things they would not normally do and went against more reasonable men's advice. You will see that in this book.

My goal is to show you how God did get involved throughout World War II. God is involved not only with individual lives, but in the affairs of all nations. The Bible says, "Daniel answered and said; Blessed be the name of God forever and ever, for wisdom and might are his. And He changes the times and seasons; He removes kings and raises up kings; He gives wisdom to the wise and knowledge to those who have understanding" (Daniel 2:20–21 NKJV).

The Bible also says, "The king's heart is in the hand of the Lord, like the rivers of water; He turns it whichever way He wishes" (Proverbs 21:1 NKJV). I believe these verses to be true, and in this book, you will see just how true they really are. I hope you enjoy it and that it will give you a greater understanding of how God works, both for us as individuals and throughout the whole world. God is there for us and will never leave us. This is a promise He gives us. "And lo I am with you always, even to the end of the age. Amen" (Matthew 28:20 NKJV).

War Begins in Europe

In the early 1930s, Germany was in the middle of the Great Depression, along with the United States and most of the Western world. The Germans were looking for help and a leader to get them out of it. Along came Adolf Hitler, just at the right time; he promised the people that they would be a great nation again.

Hitler blamed all their problems on two factors: the Jewish people in their country and the Russian communists. In 1919, Hitler joined a small group called the German Workers' Party. He was the seventh recruit and a founding member. Two years later, the party grew into thousands. He became chairman of what then became called the Nationals Sozialische Deutsche Ardeiterpartei (National Socialist German Workers' Party), also known as the Nazi Party. The party chose an ancient religious emblem, in the shape of a hooked cross; it stood for fertility and good fortune. The Nazis made it a symbol of Aryan supremacy, known as the swastika.

Hitler began his campaign by making many promises. He

would get Germany out of the Great Depression, provide jobs, stop the devaluation of the German mark, and make Germany a great power again. He could remove all the people that he believed were bringing Germany down. Many Germans believed Hitler and believed that they were betrayed in World War I. He convinced the people that the Jews were the ones who had betrayed Germany, because they wanted to stop World War I.

After four years of war and millions of dollars spent and lives lost, both sides were in agreement that the war had come to a stalemate. So on November 11, 1918, at 11:00 a.m., they proclaimed the armistice to stop the fighting. Today, November 11 is set aside as Veterans Day to thank all military personnel, past and present, for their service.

Hitler believed that if they had kept on fighting just a little longer, Germany would have been victorious. Hitler knew that he was not the only one who felt that way. He began going to beer halls throughout Germany, night after night preaching his propaganda. More and more people began to believe and follow him. The Nazi Party began to grow stronger and stronger.

On April 1, 1933, the Nazi Party began to boycott all Jewish-owned stores and shops. The Nazis burned books they believed were immoral and against their beliefs. On June 30, 1933, Adolf Hitler became chancellor of Germany. Then, on July 14, the Nazi Party became the only party in Germany. On October 14, Germany withdrew from the League of Nations. Hitler opened his first concentration camp on May 10, 1934. Then, in August 1934, Adolf Hitler become fuhrer of Germany. (Fuhrer means "supreme leader.")

Once Hitler became the head of Germany, things got completely out of control. He would not listen to anyone. He convinced the German people that they could gain control of the rest of the world through military force. He could have done things differently by building up his own country, and by listening to his advisers, engineers, generals, and admirals. Germany could have become like the United States, a world power, without force. Let me explain to you what I mean.

To gain power, Adolf Hitler looked for an enemy to conquer. On the one hand, he had the Russian Communist Party, a real threat that was planning to take over Germany. On the other hand was the German Jewish community, which was a major part of the economic, educational, scientific, and political systems. He perceived them as a threat because they were the ones holding the country together and had influence in the armistice. Hitler decided to start by destroying this perceived threat, by building concentration camps to imprison Jews, anyone who helped them, and those who did not agree with his ideas. The death camps, found by the Allies at the end of the war, had killed six million Jews and three million other people that Hitler thought were against him.

Hitler convinced the German people that they would take over all of Western Europe. His arguments were so convincing that even family members would turn against each other. Many prominent Jews in Germany realized they had to flee, so they sold their possessions and left. Among them were some of the most famous scientists.

One prominent twentieth century scientist was a man named

Albert Einstein. To get him out of Germany, US scientists devised a clever idea. They had him travel to major nations to give lectures. Hitler wanted to kill Einstein because he was Jewish. He knew Einstein's popularity would raise a lot of havoc against the Nazis, so he allowed Einstein to go on his speaking tours.

The plan was simple Einstein would speak in England and France. Then he would travel to the United States, where he would go all over the country speaking. On this tour he was well received. While he was speaking, his friends set up a house for him in Princeton, New Jersey. He then defected and became a professor of mathematics at Princeton University.

In 1940, Albert Einstein became a US citizen. He was just one of many Jewish scientists who came to the United States or Great Britain to escape the Nazis. Safe in their new countries, these people put their full efforts into defeating Hitler's Nazi Germany. These scientists were a tremendous help in the ultimate victory over Hitler.

Around the same time, another major event occurred that could have changed the course of history and propelled Germany into being the most powerful nation on earth. In 1936, a man came to Hitler with the patent for the first jet engine. His name was Hans Von Ohain. He named his patent "Process and Apparatus for Producing Airstreams for Propelling Airplanes." The Nazis were looking for more advanced technology, but Hitler did not think the jet engine would amount to anything and rejected Ohain's proposal. However, he did give Ohain some money for research and sent him on his way.

Ohain went to the Heinkel aircraft manufacturer, which

took the plans for the engine and built an airplane around it. They first built several engines, tested them, and then installed them into the aircraft. They called the aircraft the He 178. It was the world's first jet-powered airplane, flying for the first time on August 27, 1939. Hans von Ohain and Henkel contacted Herman Goring, who was the head of the German air force, known as the Luftwaffe. Hitler and Goring were getting ready to invade Poland in September 1939 but were not really interested in this aircraft. They believed that their equipment would be sufficient and superior to anyone else's military might.

Goring told Ohain he did not believe that jet aircraft would do much good for the German air force. However, Hitler and Goring gave them more money to continue working on the aircraft. Here we see a great mistake by Hitler and Goring. Can you imagine if they had invaded other countries with jet fighters and bombers leading the way? What massive destruction they could have done! No air force at that time had such aircraft. The British and Americans were working on jet engines, but they were a long way from going into production.

So what I see here is how God's hand worked on the minds of Goring and Hitler. They chose not to use this new weapon, giving the rest of the world a chance to develop it. The Germans eventually developed a fighter used in 1944, which was superior to anything the Americans or the British had. They made a few hundred of these jet aircraft, (called the Me-262,) and attacked American and British planes. Unfortunately for the Germans, it was too little, too late, because at that point, the war was just about over.

Prior to this, Germany received a lot of raw materials from Russia. However, once Adolf Hitler invaded Russia, this flow of raw materials stopped. Because of this, Germany did not have the correct materials to build these jet engines. They used a weaker material that only allowed the jet engines to run for about ten hours. Also, when the pilots took off, they had to ease the power forward slowly, because too much power would cause the engine to explode. Again, we see Hitler's folly, which we will talk more about later.

About this same time, a second scientist came to Hitler with plans for another advanced system. It was the rocket. This scientist's name was Wernher Von Braun, a leading rocket scientist of that day. He approached Hitler, asking for funds for his new weapon, even though he did not want to make weapons. He wanted to use this rocket as a vehicle for going into space. However, he knew that Hitler would not give him money for this purpose, so Von Braun's approach was to show him a new superweapon.

Again, God's hand can be seen here. The night before Hitler met with Von Braun to look at photos and movies of the new rockets, he had a nightmare about it. Although Hitler was afraid to talk to Von Braun, he had him come and politely listened to his speech, Hitler said he was interested but gave Von Braun very little money, much less than what was needed.

Hitler gave him access to a place called Peenemunde, where he could experiment with his rockets in secret. Hitler wanted nothing to do with the rocket at this time, again making a major blunder. Imagine not only having the jet plane, but also having intercontinental ballistic missiles (ICBM) in the 1930s! If he had gone to war with these weapons, there would be no telling the havoc he could have caused. Without a doubt, Hitler could have won the war with these weapons.

I believe God clouded Hitler's mind so that he would not pour billions of dollars into these weapons. Although he gave money to Von Braun to build the rockets, it was again too little, too late. With the war being almost over, Hitler had lost too many resources to manufacture many of them. There was little chance that the rockets could have helped him win the war.

In 1947 Von Braun and Von Ohain came to the United States, through an American program called Operation Paperclip. The United States Army's major function at the end of the war was to get German scientists to the United States and out of the hands of the Russians.

Von Ohain went to work for the air force at Wright–Patterson Air Force Base. In 1956 he was made the director of the Air Force Aeronautical Research Laboratory, and by 1975 he was the chief scientist of Arrow Propulsion Laboratories. He continued to contribute to the advancement of aviation and helped develop the first supersonic jet engine for the air force and navy.

Von Braun began to work for the US Army to help develop our rocket program and ICBM missiles. Von Braun developed the army's Jupiter C rocket, which was used to launch Explorer 1, the first United States satellite. He continued to work on rockets, building bigger and better ones. He developed the Saturn Five rocket, which was used to put the first men on the moon. What a fool Hitler was not to listen to these men and to let so many other scientists leave Germany!

Another major blunder Hitler made was not listening to his generals and admirals. In particular, he did not listen to Admiral Karl Donitz, who was the head admiral of Nazi Germany's submarine fleet. In the early 1930s, the German submarines were short-range. This was sufficient when they were patrolling the English Channel and around Great Britain, but they wouldn't work for the long-range targets. In 1938, Admiral Donitz told Hitler that if he would give him one or two years, he could build three hundred long-range VIIC U-boats. These U-boats were capable of sailing all the way to the United States. Admiral Donitz told Hitler that with three hundred new submarines, he could completely block the North Atlantic Ocean. No shipments from the United States, Canada, or South America could reach Great Britain.

Here again we see Hitler's folly. Although Hitler told Admiral Donitz to build those new submarines, he did not wait for them to be built before they went to war. If he had, the United States, Canada, or any other country in the Americas could not have provided Great Britain, France, or Russia with needed supplies. Hitler believed German submarines around Great Britain would be able to stop the US supplies.

At the beginning of the war, the German submarines did cost the United States and Great Britain many ships, supplies, and lives. Hitler did not have enough submarines for the duration of the war. As new technology progressed, the Allies could track down and destroy those submarines.

If Hitler had listened to and waited for Admiral Donitz to

build his new submarines, it would have been tragic for the free world. If he had that many long-range submarines, he could have literally blockaded the Americas. While Hitler did let Admiral Donitz continue building these boats, again, it was too little too late.

When the United States entered the war, and joined England in the around-the-clock bombing of German cities and factories, Germany was unable to produce the needed submarines. As the Allies began to take over France and all the other Europe countries, there was no place to build or house their submarines.

I do see God's hand in all of this, though. God clouded Hitler's mind so that he would not listen to all those brilliant men around him. The Bible says, "The king's heart is in the hand of the Lord, like the rivers of water; He turns it wherever He wishes" (Proverbs 21:1 NKJV).

Of course, Hitler was not completely in his right mind from the start, but he was still smart enough to take over Germany and then all of Western Europe in just a few months. That is why God had to intervene.

Hitler's conquest of Western Europe began on March 7, 1936. German troops occupied the Rhineland, and no one did anything. On March 12, 1936, Germany took control of Austria, and no one did anything. By March 15, 1939, German troops had taken over Czechoslovakia, and still no one did anything. On May 22, 1939, Germany signed the pact that was called the "Pact of Steel" with Italy. On August 22, 1939, Germany and Russia signed a nonaggression pact, which, of course, Hitler broke in June 1941.

Not too long after the signing of the Russian pact, on September 1, 1939, Hitler invaded Poland. The Polish army fought bravely, but with outdated equipment and outnumbered troops, it was a lost cause. It did not take long for Germany to defeat Poland's army, only twenty-nine days. On September 29, 1939, Poland fell to the German army. England and France had no choice but to declare war on Germany, and World War II in Europe officially began.

The United States, meanwhile, wanted to stay neutral in this new Western European war. On November 17, 1939, the Soviets invaded Poland; then, on November 30, the Soviets attacked Finland. Finland surrendered in March 1940. Finland signed a peace treaty with the Soviets on April 9, 1940. The Nazis invaded Denmark and Norway on May 10, 1940. At the same time, Germany invaded France, Belgium, Luxembourg, and the Netherlands.

Winston Churchill became Great Britain's prime minister on May 10, 1940. The fighting in Belgium was taking its toll on the British, French, and Belgian troops. The speed at which the Germans pushed these troops back was overwhelming. The whole world could not believe how fast Germany took over Western Europe. The Germans pushed the Allies all the way back to a small seaport on the coast of France called Dunkirk. Over three hundred thousand British and French troops were surrounded by one million German troops. No one knew what was going to happen next. In the next chapter, we are going to explore the miracle of Dunkirk.

2

Miracle at Dunkirk

fter taking Poland, between September 1939 and May 1940, not much had happened in the war. It was called the phony war because both sides were preoccupied with war preparations. On May 10, 1940, Hitler told his commanders to attack Belgium. Through the Netherlands, the German army advanced into Belgium and France. This was called "The Battle of France." The Allies fought bravely, but it was as bad as the Polish defeat. To be honest, it wasn't much of a battle.

The German army just swept through Belgium and France. The French, British, and Belgian forces were not well trained or connected. They could not coordinate their troops, so it didn't take long before the Germans had captured or killed many of the Allied troops. Every time the Allies made a counterattack, they lost more men and were pushed back even farther. Before too long, the Germans had pushed the Allied forces to a small area in France, known as the Port of Dunkirk.

They were backed up at Dunkirk, with the Germans all around them on land and with the English Channel behind them.

It did not look good for the Allies at all; they were about to lose their entire army. The British, French, and Belgian people would have no soldiers left to fight the Germans unless something was done quickly. Belgium believed it was hopeless and decided to surrender to the Germans before it lost all its young soldiers.

Then, for some unknown reason, Hitler stopped and held his forces from finishing off the Allied armies at Dunkirk. Historians, looking at this, had several theories as to why Hitler stopped. One was that the German forces moved so fast that their equipment could not hold up under so much punishment. Some of the equipment did break down, as this was the 1940s, and vehicles back then needed a lot more maintenance than they do today.

Another reason was the speculation that Field Marshal Karl Von Rundstedt, who was commanding all the armored units, was told to halt so the infantry could catch up. One other idea was that they thought the heavy equipment, the tanks and trucks, would not be able to get through the very slippery sand of Dunkirk beaches. But whatever the reason, for three days the German army did not move. Except for the artillery rounds that the British and Germans fired at each other, not much was happening.

At the same time, Field Marshal Hermann Goring, commander in chief of the Luftwaffe (air force), said his air force could destroy the Allies. After all, the Allies were surrounded and could not move. Hitler thought it would be a good idea. It would save both his men and tanks. After the war, Von Rundstedt said that the order to stop his advance was "an incredible blunder" and blamed Hitler for it. By not attacking for three days, this gave the Allies an opportunity to start getting their troops out of Dunkirk.

There were over three hundred thousand men trapped there; however, the Allies' transports, destroyers, and cruisers were too big to get close to the beach. They had some lifeboats and started pulling troops off the beaches with them. This would take many days, and the Germans were not going to wait much longer to attack. They needed more small boats to transport the troops out to the large ships.

On May 29, the order was given to the German army to attack the British Forty-Fourth Army Division at Poperinge, which was just outside of Dunkirk. If this attack had been successful, it would have cut off the Third and the Fiftieth Divisions as well. These divisions were cut off from the rest of the Allies during the retreat, but for some unknown reason, the order to attack was not carried out. The Germans did not move, and all three British divisions were able to make it to Dunkirk. Many of the German generals were upset with Hitler for ordering them to stop when they could have finished off the Allies' army. Whatever Hitler's reason, they had to obey the orders.

As I said before, the Bible says God can change men's hearts and minds. "The King's heart is in the hand of the Lord, like the rivers of water; He turns it wherever He wishes" (Proverbs: 21:1 NKJV). If Hitler had left the fighting to the army and had the air force support them, the Allies would have been destroyed at Dunkirk. Can you see how God stepped in and changed Hitler's mind?

God did not just stop there; He stepped in once more. Before the German air force could get started in its attack, there was another delay. The weather was not cooperating. It was cloudy and overcast over Dunkirk. Most of the time, the visibility was limited. Sometimes the planes could not even get off the ground. This happened throughout the entire time of the evacuation. Was it a coincidence? Of the nine days that it took to evacuate the troops from Dunkirk, there were only two and half days of clear weather; all the rest were overcast and rainy with poor flying conditions. The Royal Air Force (RAF) also had its troubles because of the weather, but the navy could and did get through this kind of weather.

Needing more small boats, Prime Minister Winston Churchill made a call throughout England. He called for anyone who had a boat long enough and big enough to cross the English Channel to France. Thousands of unarmed civilians with boats responded without hesitation. They crossed the channel and reached the beaches. Troops were loaded onto their boats and taken out to the main ships, sitting off the coast. These little boats shuttled back and forth as shells from the artillery and tanks exploded around them and even bombs from the German Luftwaffe when they could fly.

Despite attack after attack, the small boats never gave up. They continued delivering the men to the main ships, which would take them back to England. The destroyers, cruisers, and freighters dropped the troops off in Britain and then headed back for more. This method of shuttling men back and forth from France to England continued for the entire nine days.

The weather played a major role in keeping the enemy from attacking and destroying the Allied army. The miracle was getting over three hundred thousand troops out of France and back to England. Some of them were French, and some were from other countries, but the majority were English. They lost, however, much of their equipment trucks, tanks, artillery, and provisions, but the troops survived.

There's an old saying in England: "He who fights and runs away lives to fight another day." This was so true for the British army.

They fought bravely, but they were outnumbered by the Germans, so they had to run away and live to fight another day, and fight they did.

They got back to England to rearm and prepare to do battle again. This time it was to defend England from the Germans, whom they believed would be coming. With three hundred thousand trained soldiers, and the soldiers in training in England, the army, together with the civilians, began to build up the country's defenses and was ready for the attack.

Before Hitler could cross the channel, he needed to get rid of the Britain RAF. Like the outnumbered troops in Dunkirk, his troops would be under attack from the RAF, especially those sitting in barges in the open water. Hitler had now completely overrun Western Europe. But to finish the job of capturing all of Europe, Hitler had to take on Great Britain. Now that the battle for France was over, next came the Battle of Britain.

3

Battle of Britain

After the evacuation of Dunkirk, Hitler was not quite ready to launch an air attack against Great Britain. In order to destroy the RAF, the Germans needed to set up a series of fighter and bomber bases all along the coast of France. This would take approximately two months, as Hitler needed to collect tugs and barges to tow his troops across the English Channel.

This delay gave the British time to build up their bases along the coast of England. They divided their defense forces into several groups. The No. 11 Group was along the coast, the No. 12 Group was on the other side of London in the center of England, No. 10 Group was on the west side of London, and the No. 13 Group was in the northern parts of England. The No. 11 Group would receive the biggest brunt of the battle at first, because the Germans would come across the English Channel. The fighter planes had to be on the alert twenty-four hours a day to be able to get in the air within a couple of minutes.

On May 10, the Battle of Britain began in earnest. German

bombers attacked the airfields of No.11 Group and the radar stations along the coast. They sent out Stuku dive bombers to destroy the radar stations. Unfortunately for the Stukus, the British Spitfires and Hurricanes were much more maneuverable. It wasn't long before most of the Stukus were destroyed, so the German High Command took them out of the battle. Meanwhile, large formations of German medium bombers with fighter cover began attacking the British airfields along the coast.

Although the British did not have as many fighters as the Germans, they had an advantage. The German ME-109 fighter planes did not have as much fuel and could not stay with the bombers very long. So the British concentrated on the bombers and took out many of them, which was not what the Germans had expected.

Eagle Day (what Hitler called this attack) did not go well because many of the German airfields did not receive the order to attack. This is an interesting fact, as they were planning this attack for weeks, so one would think that they would have had everything in place. The other problem the Germans faced was that some airfields experienced bad weather. Planes could not get into the air. This is also strange, because they should have checked the weather forecasts.

Even though the first day did not go as planned, the Germans kept up the pressure by continuing their air raids day after day. Every day these attacks took a great toll on the men and the aircraft of both sides. The English suffered the most. The airfields were so damaged that their fighters couldn't get up into the air or down after the air battle. Vice Air Marshal Parks, who was in charge of the No. 11 Group, began to get a little worried. If this kept up for a few more days, he would have no airfields or any aircraft left to defend England.

This is when another strange thing happened that changed the entire battle. On the night of August 25, 1940, a group of German bombers were on their way to destroy some oilfields southwest of London. It was a dark night with no moon, which was good for them because it would be hard for the English gunners to spot them. The lead navigator estimated the time that they should be over their target. Because it was so dark without the moon, and all the lights on the ground were turned off, he could not see where he was flying.

During the war, cities had what were called "blackouts." At night, cities turned off street lights, and cars covered up most of their headlights (except for just a small part of the light so other vehicles could see them). Also, people had very heavy dark curtains on their windows so no light could be seen from the street. All this was so enemy planes flying over would have a hard time seeing their targets on the ground.

Unbeknownst to the Germans, the wind had shifted and pushed them more northward, as well as slowing them down. The navigator, who led the bomb group, looked for landmarks, but he couldn't see anything.

Suddenly, bright lights from the ground spotted them and flack (pieces of metal from exploding antiaircraft shells) exploded all around and buffeted them. The lead pilot asked the navigator where London was. The navigator guessed it was to the north and should be behind them by now. The lead pilot assumed they must be over some military installation because they were being shot at. He told his bombardier to drop their bombs and get out of there, and the other planes followed suit.

As it happened the next day, they found that the bomber group had been over the south end of London and not over a military installation. Up until this time, Hitler and Prime Minister Winston Churchill had a quasi-agreement that the cities would not be bombed. When Churchill saw that London had been bombed, he ordered Bomber Command to attack Berlin.

The next night, British bombers headed for Berlin. This outraged Hitler. In a speech he said, "If they drop one hundred pounds of bombs on us, we will drop one thousand pounds of bombs on them. If they drop one thousand pounds of bombs on us, we will drop ten thousand pounds on them. If they drop ten thousand pounds of bombs on us, we will drop one hundred thousand pounds of bombs on them until we have destroyed London."

He ordered the Luftwaffe to stop the airfield attacks and concentrate on London. This was his biggest mistake. The Luftwaffe's Me-109 fighter planes that were escorting the bombers to London now had only ten minutes over the target because London was so much deeper into English territory. German fighters would have to return to France before the bombers were able to finish their bombing runs over London. This opened up a much better defensive system for the British.

Vice Air Marshal Leigh-Mallory, commander of No. 12

Group, had what he called his "Big Wing," which had over one hundred airplanes. It was designed to protect London and all the other airfields, while the other fighter groups were fighting over the English Channel. When the German planes flew over London, No. 12 Group could form up and attack.

As the German planes tried to leave London with No. 12 Group on their tail, No. 10 and No. 11 Groups would come up and attack the German planes over the coast. About four times as many planes attacked the Germans, because all three groups were attacked at once. Without their fighter protection, the German bombers were at the mercy of the RAF.

Field Marshal Goering was very upset by the enormous loss of men and aircraft. When his officers tried to explain to him what was happening, he would not listen. He ordered more fighters to protect the German bombers. German fighter pilots knew more aircraft would be at the mercy of the RAF. Normally, German fighters flew much higher than the bombers. They would be free to look for the RAF and attack them from above. With Goering's order, they would have to fly lower and slower with the bombers. The Royal Air Force could come down from above and attack.

In the meantime, Vice Air Marshal Parks rebuilt the No. 11 Group's planes and airfields, and increased the number of pilots. The whole dynamic of the Battle of Britain had now changed. Before the RAF was losing; now it was beginning to win. Due to the RAF's nightly bombing runs, Berlin was directly feeling the effects of the war.

Shortly thereafter, Hitler realized he could no longer invade

England by sea and land. By September 1940, he called off the invasion, yet continued to drop bombs on London and other sites. They bombed at night to lessen the chance of attack by the RAF fighters. The war would continue for a long time; however, England now had the upper hand.

If Hitler had not stopped attacking the airfields, he would have destroyed the RAF. However, because he changed his tactics and started bombing London, he lost his opportunity for a land invasion. The great tragedy was the loss of so many innocent civilian lives. If God had not influenced Hitler to change his tactics, the Germans would have taken out the RAF and invaded Great Britain. God only knows how many innocent civilians would have died at the hands of the Nazis as they moved through Great Britain, in comparison to those who were lost in London alone. We saw how many innocent civilians died when the Nazis took over Western Europe.

It was obvious to me that God stepped in at the right time to stop the Nazis from taking over Great Britain. He caused the wind to push the German planes over London, and the whole picture of the war changed in favor of the Allies. While God does not like war, He did not want a tyrant like Hitler to win. Only He knows what would have happened if Hitler had taken over Great Britain. However, we do know that if England had been taken over, it would have been much harder, if not impossible, for the Allies to take back Western Europe.

The Battle of Britain aftermath was that the Germans lost many of their aircraft. They lost 1,636 aircraft, (47 percent of their Me-109s, 66 percent of their Me-110s, and 45 percent of their bombers). Even worse was the loss of thousands of trained airmen, who were either killed or taken prisoner. Germany never recovered from these losses, which was evident when they moved into Russia in June 1941.

England, on the other hand, recovered from its losses with the United States' assistance. The English continued to stay strong and fought on until the United States joined in the war. Hitler changed his mind from attacking the RAF airfields to bombing London just at the most crucial time in the Battle of Britain. This change brought about the ruin of the German air force. Remember what Proverbs 21:1 says, "God turns the king's heart wherever He wishes," and Daniel 2:21: "He removes kings and rises up kings" (NKJV). God is in control.

After losing the Battle of Britain, Hitler devised a plan to destroy the British infrastructure and their morale. First, Hitler continued the London air raids, which became known as the blitz. Second, he would destroy St. Paul's Cathedral, one of the most powerful icons in the city of London.

4

Bombing of St. Paul's Cathedral

On September 7, 1940, Hitler began his *Blitzkrieg* (continual night bombing runs on the London area) in earnest. He hoped, by continual bombing, that the British people would finally come to terms and sue for peace. He was wrong. In turn, it strengthened their resolve to fight.

England had many historic buildings, especially in London. Many were very flammable. In the heart of London was St. Paul's Cathedral. Its towering structure could be seen from almost anywhere in the city and had stood for hundreds of years. The minister who had charge of St. Paul's Cathedral knew that the cathedral and surrounding buildings were made of old brick and wood. Knowing they were very susceptible to fire, he organized a fire brigade and posted men around it. Water tanks were stored in the basement, in case the city's water supply was unavailable.

On September 7, now known as Black Saturday, thousands of bombs rained down on London's east end docks. No one in London had any idea what the major target of the bombardment was going to be. Walter Matthews, one of the men who were watching the bombs fall, said, "It's the end of the world."

The bombs fell on all sides of St. Paul's Cathedral. This was the first introduction to the many months of bombing to come. Yet all through the bombing, the cathedral was never touched, except for a few small bombs landing nearby causing minor damage.

On September 12, a bomb just missed the southwest tower and penetrated the pavement outside the cathedral but failed to explode. The cathedral was closed for days until the bomb could be extracted. If this bomb had gone off, its explosive power, coupled with the gas line beneath the street, would have caused serious damage. But as I said, it did not go off.

The blitz continued all through the rest of the year until Christmas 1940. There was a slight lull in the bombings for the Christmas season. But on the night of December 29, 1940, Hitler decided to concentrate his attacks on St. Paul's Cathedral. In previous bombings, his focus was not particularly on St. Paul's. Because of its importance to the Church of England, St. Paul's Cathedral was a major icon. Now was his chance to destroy the British morale by sending a large group of bombers to attack with incendiary bombs.

Incendiary bombs were not very big by themselves, about twenty-four inches long and two inches in diameter. These were tied together in groups of ten or so. Hitler sent hundreds of fully loaded bombers, each capable of carrying eleven hundred sticks of incendiary bombs. When they were dropped, the bombs would come apart, and each stick would come down on its own. When they hit something, they would start to burn and set anything they hit on fire.

Hitler hoped that burning St. Paul's Cathedral to the ground would weaken the British morale. For hundreds of years it had withstood many disasters, such as earthquakes, fires, violent storms, etc., but it had only suffered minor damage each time. Hitler reasoned that if he directly attacked the cathedral itself and burned it to the ground, he would show that nothing could stop him.

At 4:30 p.m. on December 29, German bombers arrived over London with their deadly incendiary bombs. The lead planes came in at twenty thousand feet, found St. Paul's Cathedral, and released their bombs. As the incendiaries came down, the bombs seemed to spread out in all directions, missing the cathedral, which confused the bombardiers.

Other bombers came in, and the same thing happened; all the bombs missed. Some bombers flew in from different directions, hoping the wind had caused them to miss, but the bombs still fell outside the cathedral. None fell directly on it. It was as if something was covering and protecting it.

It is important to remember that the Germans were not ignorant people. As established earlier, their scientists are known to be some of best in the world (as well as their engineers, mathematicians, physicists, etc.) The bombsights (sighting devices for aiming bombs) were not crude. They were highly technical instruments, which calculated the size and weight of the bomb, its drift, wind direction, and speed. In addition, it factored in the aircraft's speed, direction, and density of the atmosphere around it. The German bombsight was as sophisticated as the Norden bombsight used by the US Army Air Corps. Once the bomb was released, it would hit its target with high accuracy. On past bombing raids, it had done exactly that. A few strayed, but the majority hit the intended targets.

As the bombs came down, they fell away from St. Paul's Cathedral, lighting raging fires all around it. They set fire to all the surrounding buildings. The watchtower personnel saw the fires creep forward on all four sides and stop roughly twenty-five feet from the cathedral. The watchmen were afraid that the fires would leap across and totally engulf the cathedral, but they stopped on the opposite side of the street. All around the cathedral, fires were destroying every building, but none of the fires touched the cathedral itself.

When the bombers returned home, the crews tried to explain what happened. Perhaps their altitude was just too high. The German commanders told them to go in lower, at ten thousand feet this time, so that there would be very little chance of the bombs falling away. On the second bombing mission, hundreds of planes came in at ten thousand feet. Just as before, they targeted the cathedral and released their bombs. The exact same thing happened! The bombs drifted off to the side. They could not hit the cathedral. The rest of the surrounding city was in flames. The German pilots said they could see the cathedral from the light of the flames. These bombing raids continued until just before sunrise, but they still did not hit St. Paul's Cathedral.

Hitler was outraged that his prime target was not destroyed, regardless of the fact that much of London was in flames. He ordered his planes to go back in the daylight at an even lower altitude to ensure the cathedral would be destroyed. As the bombers were refueling and rearming for their third strike, something very strange happened. The weather changed, and a dense fog came in, preventing the planes from taking off. Hitler was furious; he could not believe what was happening.

Many square miles of London were in flames, hundreds of people had lost their lives, and thousands of buildings were destroyed. However, the cathedral stood and was virtually untouched, except for two incendiaries that landed on the roof's dome. One slid down the side and was quickly extinguished by the fire brigade. The other hit the top of the dome and ignited. However, before the firemen could reach it, it soundly went out all on its own. This was very strange because once the incendiaries are lit, it is very hard to put them out. They will burn until all of their fuel is used. It was very strange that of all the tens of thousands of incendiaries to drop that night, the one landing on the dome did not have enough fuel to cause any harm.

The morning after the bombing, people walked the smoke-filled streets and saw, to their joy, that the cathedral was standing and not destroyed. There is a very famous picture of the cathedral, with smoke billowing up on all sides, and there, in the middle, it stood, untouched.

The December 29 attack was not the last of the bombings of London and other British cities. The bombings continued until May 1, 1941. Despite additional attempts, the cathedral was never touched. (Google "St. Paul's Cathedral the Blitz" to see many amazing pictures of the cathedral during that time.) In May 1941, Germany prepared to attack Russia, requiring Hitler to move his bomber force from France to the Russian border. Very few bombs fell on England from that point on.

Was all this just a coincidence, and were the people of London just lucky? I do not think so. The technology had proven to be excellent up until that point. German bombers hit their target at least 90 percent of the time. Thousands of bombs fell and could not hit the target. I believe God allowed this to happen so people could see His power.

The bombing of St. Paul's Cathedral, in my mind, clearly shows that God had His hand in this. Why else would the cathedral not have been destroyed while much of London was burned to the ground? Obviously, it is up to you to make up your own mind. What do you think was happening here?

5

Germany and Italy Move into North Africa

While Hitler was gaining power in Germany in the early 1930s, another dictator was making his moves in Italy. The Fascist leader of Italy was Benito Mussolini; he came to power in 1922. Mussolini had dreams of making a great world power where ancient Rome was two thousand years earlier. While events were taking place in Western Europe, all around Italy, Mussolini saw his chance. He decided to attack Ethiopia. Ethiopia was just a small country and very poor, and Mussolini believed his air force and army could easily take it over. In 1935 he invaded Ethiopia, claiming they were taking over in a border dispute between Italian Somaliland and Ethiopia. Of course, this was a trumped-up charge to give the Italians a reason to invade.

There was some noise from the League of Nations, England, and the United States about the invasion, but nobody did anything about it. One reason was that a lot was going on in the rest of the Western world, such as Hitler making his moves and grabbing up more land in Europe. With his success in conquering

Ethiopia, Mussolini still wanted to expand his power, so he invaded Albania on April 7, 1939. As in Ethiopia, it was a very short war because Albania was not very well equipped. In September 1939, Hitler invaded Poland, and World War II started in Western Europe. Mussolini was afraid of France and was watching what was going on there. He did not declare war as soon as Hitler wanted him to, but waited until June 1940, when he could see that France and England were in big trouble.

When Mussolini declared war, both Germany and Italy began to look at the English and French colonies in North Africa. These colonies were now weakened by the war. Many of the French and British troops stationed there were called to fight in France. While the Battle of Britain was going on, Hitler was also aware of the island of Malta, located in the Mediterranean. It had an airfield and harbors that were controlled by the British.

From this island, the British sent out submarines and planes to attack German convoys coming into the Mediterranean. So Hitler laid siege to the island of Malta on June 11, 1940. The siege lasted longer than Hitler anticipated. It lasted until November 20, 1942, and he never did gain control of the island of Malta. Since Hitler had taken over all of Western Europe, Mussolini, desiring Italy to be a great nation again, decided to move his army into North Africa and Greece.

In October 1940, Mussolini invaded Greece. Hitler was unsure if Mussolini was capable of taking Greece. Greece was allied with the British. Hitler believed if he could neutralize Greece, it would protect him from a British invasion from that part of the world. Therefore, Hitler did not try to stop

Mussolini from invading Greece. Italy attacked, and it was a disaster. The Italians severely underestimated the Greeks' fighting capability. In addition, the British sent in more troops to help defend the Greeks.

Mussolini asked Hitler to send German troops to Greece. However, Hitler's generals were against it. They felt they needed to concentrate on invading Russia and not waste troops on these little Mediterranean islands. Hitler, as he had done so many times before, did not listen to his generals. With the help of the German army, Greece was soon overwhelmed and captured by the Italians in April 1941. Some of the British troops in Greece retreated to the island of Crete. It did not take long for German paratroopers to take the island of Crete, as well.

Hitler attacked Greece by bombing Cyprus. Hitler thought he could do this in just a few months, but the British put up a very good fight. The Greek and the British troops, who had moved from Greece to Crete, pushed back the Italian army and decimated many German paratroopers. As more German paratroopers arrived, they finally captured the airfield.

It wasn't too long before Crete fell. Even though Hitler's attack on Crete was successful, the loss of so many paratroopers bothered him greatly. He believed they were ineffective in a major offensive. They could have been used more effectively throughout the war and perhaps changed the course of some future battles. Here again, we see how God changed the minds of these generals and leaders to do things they normally wouldn't do. This forced them to lose battles, as we will see later on in this book.

While the Germans fought in Greece, the Italians prepared to take North Africa. In June 1940, the Italians attacked the British troops in Libya and Egypt. The Italians captured British Somaliland and made incursions into Kenya. In December 1940, the British, with a force of thirty thousand men, attacked the Italians, with over two hundred thousand troops in Egypt. The British thought this would be just a quick battle to regain some territory. As they successfully pushed the Italians back farther and farther, they chose to continue the offensive. In several weeks, they crossed Egypt and took thousands of Italian prisoners. By February 1941, the British had advanced over five hundred miles with very minor losses, so they attacked Eastern Africa to retake Somaliland and Ethiopia.

It was very strange that thirty thousand British troops could beat back two hundred thousand Italian troops. Maybe it is not so strange, since God can pull down nations. "The instant I speak concerning a nation and concerning a kingdom, to pluck up, to pull down, and to destroy it" (Jeremiah 18:7 NKJV).

England had North African colonies. This was an opportunity to fight the Germans in that part of the world, as well as attempt to take the pressure off of them in Western Europe. The British moved troops into North Africa to fight the Germans, sending their best general, General Bernard Montgomery, and his Eighth Army.

With few German troops in North Africa and the Italians forces crumbling, Hitler had little choice but to send in a larger force, of over five hundred thousand troops. They were led by one of his most brilliant generals, Field Marshal Erwin

Rommel, who later gained a reputation as the "Desert Fox." Rommel arrived in Tripoli on February 12, 1941, and in April began attacking the British forces. The Germans began to take back Libya and then moved on to the Suez Canal. Rommel requested more troops to complete his objective. Once again, we see the folly of Adolf Hitler. He was very obsessed with attacking Russia. Instead of crushing the British in North Africa, he did not send Rommel the needed troops. For the rest of the year, the British and German forces attacked, pushing each other back and forth. It became a stalemate.

North Africa became a sideshow compared to what was happening in Europe. The sideshow drained troops and supplies. It kept one of Hitler's greatest generals occupied when he was needed in Russia. North Africa became Hitler's Achilles' heel. He pulled troops and equipment from the Russia invasion, but he did not send enough troops to North Africa. Hitler's army was unable to totally control the Middle East and the Mediterranean Sea. When the United States joined the fight in North Africa, there was no way Germany could win. It delayed his invasion of Russia until June 1941 and tied up troops in North Africa for two years. I believe we can see God's hand at work. God interfered, by clouding Hitler's mind. Instead of focusing on one objective, he moved troops from the Russian border to North Africa, thus delaying his attack into Russia. We will see how this delay and distraction would eventually cost Hitler the war.

6

Germany Invades Russia

While the North African war continued, Hitler planned to invade Russia in May 1941; however, the North African campaign delayed his invasion until June. This caused Hitler to lose, not only the war in Russia, but the entire war. As we progress, you'll see what I mean.

Along the Russian border, Hitler had amassed over four million men, thousands of vehicles, airplanes, and tons of supplies. He believed that his men would sweep through Russia, completing his invasion by December. Why wouldn't he think this? He had captured all of Western Europe in about eight months.

One mistake was that he wanted to attack using three different army groups: one attacking northern Russia, another attacking Moscow, and the last attacking the southern part of Russia. His generals argued that they needed all the troops to capture Moscow first. This would demoralize the Russian people and make it easier to capture the rest of the nation. Hitler believed his plan was right and would not listen to his generals.

Field Marshall Rommel and a half million of his troops were

in North Africa. Some of Hitler's generals believed they should not attack Russia at all, but focus on knocking out the Allies (especially the British) in North Africa. After its loss in the 1940 Battle of Britain, Germany never was able to invade Great Britain after it took Western Europe. Now was the Germans' chance to eliminate the British army without invading England.

Again, Hitler would not hear of it. He hated Russia more than any other country in the world. Russia had natural resources that Germany desperately needed. On June 22, 1941, Hitler launched his massive attack. At first, all was going well for the German army. They had a huge front and were making great progress through the Russian countryside. Hitler believed that they would capture Moscow, Leningrad, and the southern part of Russia by the end of September.

I believe this thinking is where God got involved. The Bible says; "The King's heart is in the hand of the Lord, Like the rivers flow; He turns it wherever He wishes" (Proverbs 21:1 NKJV). This includes dictators and generals.

God controls the weather. Winter came early in 1941. "Now when Jesus got into a boat, His disciples followed Him. And suddenly a great tempest arose on the sea, so that the boat was covered with the waves. But He was asleep. Then His disciples came to him and awoke Him, saying, 'Lord, save us! We are perishing!' But He said to them, 'Why are you fearful, O you of little faith?' Then He arose and rebuked the winds and the sea. And there was a great calm. And the men marveled, saying, 'Who can this be, that even the winds and the sea obey Him?'" (Matthew 8:23–27 NKJV).

The rain came down in torrents, and the German vehicles ground to a halt. The roads were nothing but mud, and the trucks, tanks, and other vehicles could not move. Without their mechanized vehicles, the German army was in very big trouble. Meanwhile, the Russians were accustomed to this type of weather and knew how to maneuver. The German army faced another obstacle. Joseph Stalin, the dictator of Russia, ordered a scorched earth policy. This policy was very simple. As the Germans advanced, the Russian people and soldiers destroyed anything they could not take with them: homes, buildings, railroads, and crops. This left the Germans with no food or shelter.

This policy was very effective. The Nazi army had to rely on supplies coming in from Germany. In Western Europe, the railroads were built on the same gauge so people and goods could be moved from one country to another with relative ease. In Russia, however, each province had its own rail gauge size. When people moved from one province to the next, they got off at a train station and boarded a train with different rail gauge.

When the German trains first arrived in Russia, it was no problem. When they got deeper into Russia, the train tracks were the wrong size for the German trains. The Germans had to unload cargo from their own trains and locate usable trains. Now remember, the scorched earth policy destroyed most of those railcars, locomotives, and tracks, so that the Germans could not use them. They had to either use their own trucks to move their cargo or repair the train tracks and Russian trains. This, of course, took a lot of time.

Another problem the Nazis faced was Russia's immense size. It was seven hundred miles into Russia as the crow flies, but by truck or tank, it was fifteen hundred miles. The snow came early that year as well. The first snowfall was on October 6. This was one of the earliest and coldest winters in Russian history. Weather conditions and poor equipment caused the Germans to reach Moscow in December rather than September. How strange that the worst winter ever hit just when the German army invaded Russia. No doubt God had stepped in.

Russian winters are much harsher than winters in Germany, or in Western Europe, for that matter. The Germans were unprepared for such conditions. The German army only had summer clothing. In their arrogance, they believed they would be in Moscow by September. So now troops were freezing, and food was becoming scarce. Hitler had not anticipated the huge amount of countryside that they would have to travel. The distance from the Russian border to Moscow was almost the same length as all of Western Europe. The German army could see Moscow but could not advance because of the rough winter and lack of supplies.

Meanwhile in Moscow, the Russians built barricades while the Germans were stalled. They brought in Siberian troops, who were very used to the cold, and continued fighting the Germans throughout the winter. The Germans were stopped, and the Russians kept up the attack. The Russian gasoline-powered tanks and vehicles could move in the winter cold easily, like most of our automobiles today. The German vehicles had diesel engines, which have a rough time in very cold climates. Fires were lit under the diesel truck engines and tanks to warm them up so they would start. This poses a real problem when under attack, and vehicles are needed immediately.

Hitler's Army Group South, which was fighting in the Ukraine, was having a very difficult time. Hitler ordered several divisions to move from Army Group Center, which was attacking Moscow, to aid them. This weakened the troops attacking Moscow until winter ended in March 1942.

Meanwhile, Army Group North was advancing on Leningrad, believing they would be able to capture it before the end of December. This was not to be, because the bad winter weather hit them as well. They surrounded Leningrad, which began a nine-hundred-day siege that Hitler and the German army were not prepared for. They never got past Moscow and Leningrad.

Not only was the winter affecting the tanks and trucks, it was also affecting the German air force. The temperature was very cold, and it was difficult to start the planes. The upper-level weather was cloudy, foggy, and turbulent, making it difficult to fly and find targets on the ground.

Hitler lost in Russia because the skillful Russians could tear down a factory, move it hundreds of miles, and have it fully running again in six weeks. This made it hard for Germans to destroy Russian manufacturing capabilities. With the Allies shipping in raw materials, the Russians continued producing arms and supplies to send to their troops.

Another great mistake was that Hitler assumed the Japanese would join forces with Germany. In December 1941, Japan attacked the United States by bombing Pearl Harbor. War was declared between the two countries. Hitler believed if he joined forces with Japan against the United States, then Japan would join him in fighting against the Russians. This belief came from a pact that Germany had with Japan, but Hitler had forgotten a very important detail. The pact stated that if a nation invaded one of their countries, the other one would join forces to fight off the invader. In the case of Pearl Harbor, Japan attacked the United States, not the other way around. When Hitler asked Japan to help him fight Russia, Japan said, "No, we fought the Russians in 1905. We beat them on the ocean but fought to a stalemate on land. We do not need a two-front war right now because we are already fighting the Chinese and the Americans."

Hitler's major downfall was declaring war on the United States. If Hitler had not done so, the United States may not have joined England and Russia in fighting the Germans. The United States may have sent more supplies to England and Russia, but not troops. The United States would have put all its effort toward fighting the Japanese in the Pacific.

God let Hitler think he could overtake Russia and allowed him to fall into a false sense of security. This was the beginning of the end for him. With the United States in the war, it put in millions of men and provided tons of supplies for all the Allies.

The fighting in Russia continued until February 1942, when the Germans were surrounded by the Russian army at Leningrad and had to surrender. From that point on, it became a struggle for the Nazi army to return to Germany. The winters were still harsh, and it was a long road. Supplies were few and far between. Soon Allied forces landed in France, and the Germans were stuck between the Russians in the East and the Allies in the West. It was now just a matter of time before Germany would surrender.

7

The United States Enters the War

In the late 1930s, war was raging in Western Europe and in China. Meanwhile, the United States did not want to get involved. After all, it had only been a little over twenty years since the United Stated had been involved in a war in Western Europe. There were two opposing groups in the United States. One group, known as the "isolationists," wanted to stay out of the war. The other group, sometimes call the "hawks," believed the United States needed to help the British and the Chinese. One prominent member of the hawks was President Franklin Delano Roosevelt (FDR). When Japan attacked China in the early 1930s, he requested the Japanese pull out of China. If not, he would stop sending them raw materials they wanted. When the Japanese did not pull out of China, he did just that. This enraged the Japanese, and friction began to develop over this policy. The Japanese moved into other surrounding countries to acquire the raw materials.

With this tension increasing day by day, Roosevelt decided in 1940 that the Pacific Fleet should conduct exercises around the Hawaiian Islands. Following these exercises, the fleet remained at Pearl Harbor on the island of Oahu. By mid-1941, the entire fleet was moved there on a permanent basis.

When the Japanese saw the Pacific Fleet being moved from San Diego to Pearl Harbor, it disturbed them very much. The move showed that the United States was serious by moving its fleet closer to the Japanese expansion. Soon people in both countries realized that war was going to come between them.

The United States built up its arsenal, and so did the Japanese. Due to the lack of US raw materials, the Japanese were forced to look elsewhere. Some resources were found in the South Pacific island colonies governed by the British, Dutch, and French. Because of the pact they had signed with Hitler, the Japanese hoped he would send support to fight against the Americans in the Pacific. Japan also knew that President Roosevelt was distracted by the war in Europe, and thought this was a weakness it could exploit.

At this time, President Roosevelt coined the phrase that the United States was "the Arsenal of Democracy." Since the beginning of the conflict, the United States supplied the free world with materials to defend itself.

In September 1939, Hitler started the war by invading Poland. When this happened, England and France declared war on Germany to fulfill their promise to Poland. They had a protective alliance, meaning that if one country was attacked, the others would come to its aid. In 1939, Winston Churchill became prime minister of England and began to negotiate with President Roosevelt, hoping to get foreign aid. Roosevelt said

England would have to buy it; the United States would not simply give it to the British. So convoys of British and American ships began moving materials to Great Britain. This outraged Hitler, but he refrained from attacking American ships until 1941. At that point, German U-boats began sinking American warships and cargo ships heading to England.

As the war progressed, and England's resources and funds decreased, President Roosevelt began a new program called lend-lease. The British were given the opportunity to get more war supplies on credit. Roosevelt said this was like loaning your neighbor a garden hose when his house was on fire. When Hitler attacked Russia in 1941, Stalin, Russia's dictator, wanted aid from the United States as well. The United States supplied the Russians with needed items. The Japanese watched the movements in Europe and the response by the United States. They believed the Americans would be so distracted by the war that Japan could do anything it pleased in the Pacific.

The Japanese knew they had to act fast. This task was turned over to Admiral Yamamoto, who had spent several years in the United States, studied at Harvard University, and was well versed in American culture. He was against going to war with the United States. He told his superiors that the Americans were not lazy and only interested in luxuries. They were a just and noble people, and would be a very formidable foe if Japan went to war with them. The only way to make peace would be for Japan to march into the White House and demand it. Yamamoto knew that would not happen. War would be very costly, and no doubt Japan would lose.

Yamamoto knew of only one way to get the advantage over the Americans. Japan must first destroy the United States' fleet at Pearl Harbor. The admiral devised a plan to attack the United States on a Sunday, when the fleet would be at rest in the harbor. This was going to have to be a sneak attack.

8

Japan Attacks Pearl Harbor

In the beginning of 1941, the Japanese started to plan a sneak attack on the United States. To carry out their plan, they needed six aircraft carriers and all of their planes. The main target would be the aircraft carriers at Pearl Harbor, next the battleships, and then any other ships that they could find. Admiral Nagumo was chosen to lead the task force and carry out the attack.

The Japanese task force left its home waters in November. They arrived near Pearl Harbor on Sunday, December 7, 1941. Their projected targets were the aircraft carriers. However, what they did not know was that the aircraft carriers were not at Pearl Harbor on December 7. Each carrier had been sent on a mission to deliver aircraft to other places in the Pacific. Even the newest carrier, the USS *Hornet*, was still on the East Coast going through sea trials. It was a very unusual move for the United States to have all of its carriers out at sea at the same time. I believe God had set this up so that the carriers would not be destroyed at Pearl Harbor and would be available for the battles that occurred later.

During the journey to the island of Oahu, where Pearl Harbor is located, the Japanese task force encountered a variety of weather conditions that concealed it from the United States' patrol ships and aircraft. The Japanese thought this was a good sign for them. In reality, God used this storm to keep the aircraft carrier USS *Enterprise*, from arriving in Pearl Harbor at its scheduled time, which was 7:30 a.m. Sunday, December 7. During the storm, the oilers could not refuel the *Enterprise* and its escort ships. This delayed the task force by four hours, so it arrived at Pearl Harbor after the attack.

If the *Enterprise* had arrived at Pearl Harbor on schedule, the planes would have taken off and landed at Ford's Island, leaving the carrier with no aircraft. (The aircraft take off from the carrier before it gets to the home base so that the navy planes can be used while they are in port. The planes cannot fly off the carrier when it is tied up at the dock in the harbor; the ship has to be moving.) If the *Enterprise* had arrived at Pearl Harbor on schedule, the carrier would have been blown up and its planes destroyed at the airfield.

It was daybreak on December 7, 1941, when the Japanese planes arrived over the island at approximately 7:30 a.m. Hawaiian time. The Japanese task force had launched its planes from its position (two hundred miles north of Oahu), and they came in from three different directions. This was a total surprise to the Americans. With no aircraft carriers to bomb, the next major targets were the battleships tied up at Battleship Row off

Ford Island. A Japanese bomb hit the USS *Arizona*. It took a hit in the forward magazine compartment (this is where the shells and gunpowder are stored), exploded, and immediately the ship went down, taking over twelve hundred sailors with it.

The mistake that the Japanese made in their Pearl Harbor attack was that they only concentrated on the ships. Since the aircraft carriers were not there, they attacked the battleships and other warships in the harbor instead. They neglected many areas that could have really put Pearl Harbor out of commission for years, such as the dry docks, warehouses, and fuel storage tanks. The navy would not have been able to raise and refit the ships that were sunk, nor could the harbor have been used as a base throughout the war. However, the sinking of the USS *Arizona* and other ships caused a great deal of damage, and set the navy back about a year.

The Japanese planes came from three directions: one group directly from the north, and the other two groups swinging around and coming in from east and west. This caused great confusion on the ground and onboard the ships. The Japanese planes also attacked Schofield Barracks (killing army troops there), Hickam Air Force Base, and Wheeler Airfield (damaging and destroying many aircraft on the ground).

Another ship at Pearl Harbor was USS *Neosho*, the largest oil tanker in the navy's fleet. On December 6, the *Neosho* arrived fully loaded with aviation fuel. It docked at Hickam Airfield and unloaded half of its one million gallons of aviation fuel into the storage tanks. That evening the *Neosho* cast off and headed for the docks of Ford Island, which was near Battleship Row. After it passed the *Arizona*, it docked between the USS *California* and the USS *Oklahoma*, so it was right in the middle of Battleship Row, for all intents and purposes. At 7:55 a.m., the *Neosho* was docked at Ford Island; her fuel storage tanks were about half-empty. What causes fuel, such as aviation gas, to explode? It is the fumes. With the ship's tanks half emptied, a tremendous amount of fumes was in that ship. It was the largest ship afloat for tankers.

When the Japanese attacked, the tanker was in great danger because Japanese planes were diving down on the battleships. A photo shows the *Neosho* sitting there with bombs splashing all around it. The crew manned their guns and began firing back at the Japanese planes, managing to down one plane. The situation got worse when the *Arizona* exploded near them and rocked the ship. The USS *California* and the USS *Oklahoma* were hit, and right between them was the *Neosho*. Yet the Japanese planes did not look at the tanker as a target.

This was a large mistake. The Japanese thought that destroying warships would bring the Americans to their knees. What really would have brought a great victory to the Japanese would have been to bomb the *Neosho*. If the *Neosho* had been hit, there would have been a tremendous explosion. The ship would have been destroyed. Who knows how much damage the explosion would have caused, with all the fuel onboard and its location being not far from the fuel storage tanks?

Around 8:40 a.m., there was a slight lull in the action. Captain John Phillips ordered the *Neosho* to get under way and head to a safer berth at Mirror Point, tying up behind the USS

Caster. From here the *Neosho* continued firing its guns from a safer distance than right on Battleship Row. At 9:10 a.m. the last Japanese planes left Pearl Harbor, flying back to the carriers north of Oahu.

While the attack was under way, Admiral Nagumo found out that the US aircraft carriers were not at Pearl Harbor at all. Not knowing where they were, or knowing the location of any of the United States submarines on patrol, he decided he had done enough damage and pulled around and headed back for Japan. This was another big mistake that the Japanese made. Because they did not launch the second or third attacks, they missed out on destroying the oil and gasoline storage tanks, the dry docks and warehouses, and the submarines that were sitting in the harbor.

This would have caused immense damage to the US Navy. They would have been unable to repair the ships hit in Pearl Harbor. Some might have made it back to San Diego or San Francisco, but it would have taken at least a week to get there and more time to get them repaired.

Pearl Harbor could have been in serious trouble and knocked out of the war as a major seaport for several years. At that time, everybody was in shock and was horrified by the destruction, but if those oil tanks had gone up, half of Pearl Harbor would have gone up with them.

The ships that were hit were raised because Pearl Harbor was shallow, and many of them did not completely sink. They were repaired and upgraded to 1941 standards by adding radar and sonar. (The ships were not equipped with these devices when they were attacked at Pearl Harbor.) Also newer guns were added, making them in better shape than before the Pearl Harbor attack. Things could have been much worse, but I believe God's hand was involved.

As I said before, Admiral Yamamoto knew Japan could not win the war with the United States. He hoped to inflict enough damage to force the Americans to rethink their position in the Pacific and perhaps sue for peace with Japan. The Japanese might have been able to keep their captured territory, which would give them the needed raw materials. It would have given them control and dominance over the South Pacific, but that was not to be. When the attack was over, and reports came in from Admiral Nagumo's task force, all of Japan was celebrating the victory. However, all the Pearl Harbor attack did was create much anger in the United States toward the Japanese.

Admiral Yamamoto knew this was not going to be a great victory after all. Another problem was that the standard protocol was to give a declaration of war before an attack. However, the Japanese could not translate the declaration into English and present it to Washington, DC, before the attack. Admiral Yamamoto, upon hearing the news, knew this would be a terrible blow to Japan. He knew full well how the Americans would react to such an insult. He warned his government that the United States would not tolerate insults and would fight back viciously. He was right. The Japanese paid a very high price for going to war with the United States.

Seeing how things turned out in the Pearl Harbor attack, I believe God's hand was involved. God did not stop the attack but kept the damage and the loss of life to a minimum. It could have been a lot worse for the United States. The Bible says, "But the LORD your God you shall fear; and He will deliver you from the hand of all your enemies" (2 Kings 17:39 NKJV).

9

Doolittle Raid

The war in the Pacific was raging, and the Allies were losing. On December 7, 1941, the Japanese bombed Pearl Harbor and attacked the Philippines, Wake Island, and Guam. Then on December 8, the Japanese attacked Hong Kong, causing the British to surrender ten days later. The Japanese also took Thailand, Singapore, Burma, and Malaysia.

Most of these places were under the control of Great Britain. To help stop the Japanese advance, the British sent out two of their biggest warships in the South Pacific: the battleship *Prince of Wales* and the battle cruiser *Repulse*. Both ships were sunk by Japanese aircraft shortly after getting involved in the navy campaign in the Pacific. When Winston Churchill heard the news, he said, "In all the war, I never received a more direct shock." At this point in the war, there was virtually no British navy in the Pacific.

After losing all the other Pacific bases, the only British base left was in the Philippines. By the end of December, the Japanese had taken Manila, the capital of the Philippines, and were sending more and more troops daily. They were also continually bombing all of the American positions. General Douglas MacArthur was the commander of US troops in the Philippines. He had no choice but to pull back to the Bataan Peninsula, where he hoped he could hold out until US reinforcements would arrive. The situation in the Philippines had become so desperate that on March 11, President Roosevelt ordered General MacArthur and his staff to leave and go to Australia. On May 6, the remaining forces in the Philippines surrendered to the Japanese, and the infamous Bataan Death March began.

The war in the North Atlantic and in Europe was not going well either. By June 1940, the British had to pull their troops out of France. During the famous Battle of Britain, England kept the German army from invading with the valiant efforts of the Royal Air Force. However, this was the only good news the Allies had from the Western European Front. From that point on, things had gone from bad to worse.

Germans bombers kept up the pressure by bombing London and other English cities. German U-boats, operating in the North Atlantic, continually attacked convoys coming from the United States and Canada. They sank dozens of ships that were carrying millions of tons of cargo, needed by the British and the Russians. Allied forces were taking a pounding in North Africa, and German troops were moving through Russia in record time.

With all this bad news, President Roosevelt needed something to help the morale of the American people—and fast. He met with his military advisers several times a week. Roosevelt's military advisers were General George C. Marshall, army chief of staff; General Hap Arnold, chief of staff of the Army Air Force; and Admiral Ernest J. King, chief of naval operations. President Roosevelt wanted to strike back at the Japanese as soon as possible. Each time he met with his advisers, he would ask, "Do you have a plan to bomb Japan yet?"

All three men put their staff to work on the problem. One idea was to use B-17s and B-24s, flying from Vladivostok, Siberia, but the Russians did not want to get involved in a two-front war. They were fighting the Germans in their own country, and the Russian army was taking an awful beating. Now President Roosevelt was asking them to help the United States by fighting the Japanese in China. That was not going to happen.

Roosevelt's staff also looked into having B-17s and B-24s fly from China to bomb Japan. The logistics of moving heavy bombers all the way to China was out of the question that early in the war. The bombers could not fly over Russian territory, because, as stated before, the Russians would not want to get involved with Japan. The B-17s and the B-24s did not have the range to fly all the way to China without having to land three or four times for refueling. Flying over the Pacific Ocean was out of the question because, at this point in the war, Japan controlled most of the South Pacific islands.

Captain Francis S. Low, who was on Admiral King's staff, was returning from Norfolk, Virginia, after checking on the readiness of the aircraft carrier USS *Hornet*. He noticed a carrier outline painted on the runway. It was to give navy pilots practice taking off from short distances. It was also used by both navy and army planes as a target for bombing practice. When Captain Low's plane was flying over the outline, he saw army twin-engine planes making bombing passes at the simulated carrier deck. The army planes' shadows flew right over the outline. The thought hit him: *Why can't army twin-engine planes take off from a carrier? They can carry more bombs and fly farther than navy carrier planes can.*

For only a few seconds, Captain Low's plane, the army planes, the carrier outline, and the sun were in the right position for all of it to come together at the right time. Was it only a coincidence? You think about it!

Upon his return to Washington, DC, Low went to see Admiral King. After telling the admiral his idea, King replied, "Low, you may have something there. Talk to Duncan about it in the morning." The next morning, Low met with Captain Donald B. "Wu" Duncan, Admiral King's air operations officer. They began to investigate if army planes could land on a carrier. Right away, they saw that it was impossible for army planes to land on a carrier. They did not have a tail hook to catch the cables, and the landing gear was not strong enough for a hard landing. The planes would have to be lifted up onto the carrier's deck by a crane.

The next task was to see which army plane could take off from a carrier. There were four twin-engine planes in the army inventory: the B-18, the B-23, the B-25, and the B-26. The B-18 and B-23 were old and were used only for training. The

B-26 needed too much runway to take off, and the wings were too long. The best choice was the B-25 bomber, but it would need some modifications.

Duncan and Low gave Admiral King their report. King told General Hap Arnold of the idea and sent Duncan and Low to Arnold's office. Arnold also liked the idea. He would put his best man on the army's end of the project and asked Duncan and Low to take the navy's part. General Arnold needed a man to lead this dangerous mission who was used to doing the impossible, an experienced pilot who could inspire others by example. That man, Lieutenant Colonel James H. "Jimmy" Doolittle, was right down the hall from his office.

Jimmy Doolittle was born in Alameda, California, on December 14, 1896. Doolittle served in the Army Air Corps from 1917 until 1930. He continued serving in the Army Air Corps Reserve as a major for the next ten years. In 1923, he enrolled in the Massachusetts Institute of Technology (MIT). He obtained a master's, and a PhD in aeronautical engineering in June 1925. He was the first person to receive this degree. Doolittle was also the first person to win all the major aviation racing trophies. In 1931, Doolittle went to work for Shell Oil Corporation, continuing to win more racing trophies. In 1932, he broke the world landplane speed record, flying the Bee Gee R-1 to a record speed of 406 miles per hour. He also helped in developing instruments for flying in poor weather and urged Shell Oil to increase its ability to manufacture high-octane aviation fuel. In 1940, he returned to active duty in the Army Air Corps and was promoted to lieutenant colonel.

After Doolittle reviewed Duncan and Low's plan, he was in favor of using the B-25s for the raid, but the planes needed a lot of modifications to bomb Japan and fly on to China. The modifications to the planes were called the "B-25'B Special Project." It was now the middle of January, and General Hap Arnold and Admiral King wanted the planes to be ready by April 1. General Hap Arnold gave Doolittle his top priority stamp. Doolittle said, "I was extremely unpopular everywhere I went, but with that top priority straight from the top, I got what I needed, and I got it quickly."

The plan was for a navy aircraft carrier to carry the army planes to a location within 450 miles from Japan. The navy would launch the planes over Japan at night and bomb military and industrial targets in Tokyo, Nagoya, Osaka, and Kobe. Each plane carried three five-hundred-pound demolition bombs and one pack of five-hundred-pound incendiary bombs. From Japan, they would fly to the Chengchow, China, airbase, refuel, and go on to the city of Chungking. The planes would fly over two thousand miles, which was twice the range of the B-25.

The plane modifications were major. The first item was to lighten the planes as much as possible. The secret Norden bombsight was the first to go for these reasons: (1) it was the most accurate device used at the time, and the government did not want it to fall into enemy hands; (2) it was very heavy; and (3) it was not very accurate below four thousand feet. The bombers were going to drop their bombs from fifteen hundred feet.

The radios were removed because of their weight. This

eliminated the need for a radio operator, limiting even more weight. The radio operator's compartment was then used to store ten five-gallon fuel cans. A 225-gallon fuel tank was put in the bomb bay, and a 160-gallon rubber fuel tank was put in the crawlway above the bomb bay. The lower gun turret was removed, and a sixty-gallon fuel tank was installed in its place. With the new fuel tanks and the fuel tanks already in the plane's wings, each B-25 had a total of 1,141 gallons of fuel. This was more than enough fuel to reach the Chinese airbase. To give the appearance of having two additional fifty-caliber machine guns, two broom handles were painted black and mounted in the tail of the B-25s.

Doolittle asked for twenty-four B-25s and the volunteer flight crews to report to Florida's Eglin Air Field. For the next ten weeks, the crews practiced takeoffs in less than five hundred feet, low-level flying, bombing runs from fifteen hundred feet, night flying, and navigation, all under the strictest security. If word of the mission leaked out, it would jeopardize the lives of the air crews and the navy task force ships and sailors.

With all the training and modifications completed, it was time for Doolittle and his planes to head to the West Coast to join Navy Task Force 16. Navy Task Force 16 was divided into two groups: 16.1 and 16.2. Task Force 16.2 was built around the aircraft carrier USS *Hornet*, which carried Doolittle and his planes. It had two cruisers, (the USS *Nashville* and the USS *Vincennes*); the oiler USS *Cimarron*; and the destroyers from Destroyer Division 22, the USS *Gwinn*, USS *Meredith*, USS *Grayson*, and USS *Monssen*.

Task Force 16.1 was built around the aircraft carrier USS *Enterprise*. Because the flight deck of the *Hornet* was loaded with Doolittle's planes, it was impossible for the *Hornet* to launch its own planes. The fighter *Enterprise* planes were needed for air cover. Task Force 16.1 had two cruisers (the USS *Northampton* and the USS *Salt Lake City*), the oiler USS *Sabine*, and Destroyer Division 6 with the USS *Balch*, USS *Benham*, USS *Ellet*, and USS *Fanning*. Two submarines, USS *Thresher* and the USS *Trout*, were involved in the operation. They were to lay off the Japanese coast and radio back weather conditions and what was happening in Tokyo Bay.

The *Hornet*, under the command of Captain Marc Mitscher, left the West Coast on the morning of April 2. It headed west, along the 40th parallel, and joined up with its escorts, becoming Task Force 16.1. The *Enterprise*, under the command of Admiral William F. Halsey, left Pearl Harbor with its escorts on April 7 and rendezvoused with the *Hornet* on April 12. When both Task Force 16.1 and 16.2 moved up, it was then called Task Force 16. Admiral Halsey, who was the highest-ranking officer, was now in command of Task Force 16. Before Task Force 16.1 and 16.2 joined together, they had been in radio communication. Unknown to the task force, the Japanese had broken the navy's code and were listening to their radio communications.

The Japanese learned that the United States Navy was on its way to bomb Tokyo. The task force continued to move on with little or no problem until the morning of April 18. Fog, low clouds, rough seas, and rain squalls were occurring frequently. Around daybreak, the task force was spotted by a Japanese fishing boat, part of a line of boats stationed eight hundred miles from Japan. The fishing boat was able to radio Japan before the task force sank it.

The Japanese High Command did not know that long-range bombers were on the *Hornet*. They believed that the task force would have to get within three hundred miles before they could launch an attack. They thought it should take the task force two or three days before it would be in range, giving them plenty of time to get ready for the Americans.

After being spotted by the Japanese picket boat, Admiral Halsey had no idea whether the Japanese were now planning an attack on his task force. At this time in the war, the United States had only four aircraft carriers in the Pacific. The navy was in no shape to risk losing two of its aircraft carriers and all the support ships. Admiral Halsey ordered the *Hornet* to launch Doolittle's planes as soon as possible so the task force could head back to Pearl Harbor. They were about two hundred miles farther from Japan than the plan had called for. Admiral Halsey had a signalman flash this message to the *Hornet*: "LAUNCH PLANES X TO COL DOOLITTLE AND GALLANT COMMAND GOOD LUCK AND GOD BLESS YOU."

On the *Hornet*, things were moving fast. With all the bombs loaded several days before, the planes were now being moved into takeoff position. The gas tanks were topped off as the crews climbed into their planes. Doolittle was going to be the first to take off. Everyone watched closely. If he made it, all the other crews could make it, too.

Doolittle revved the B-25's engines to maximum. H.

Newman, Doolittle's copilot, held the brakes tight and watched a man holding a checkered flag. When the man dropped the flag, Doolittle was to release his brakes and roll down the deck. The flag finally dropped, and Doolittle started down the deck. At just the right moment, Doolittle pulled back on the control wheel, and the B-25 lifted into the air.

On the deck of the *Hornet*, the men's cheers were so loud that the crews in their planes (with both engines running) easily hear them. Doolittle passed over the *Hornet* to look for a man holding a chalkboard indicating the direction to fly. All the planes took off safely, passed over the carrier, and headed for Japan. Because of the great distance, they could not waste gas circling to form up in bomber formation. Each plane was on its own and flying only twenty feet above the water.

At first, the early takeoff looked like it would jeopardize the mission. In reality, it saved the mission. Knowing that the Americans were coming, the Japanese had hundreds of land-based bombers, with a range of at least one thousand miles, waiting for the task force's carriers and destroyers to come into position.

Also patrolling off the Japanese coast were the six aircraft carriers and their escort ships that had attacked Pearl Harbor. If the task force had reached the Doolittle bombers' previously planned takeoff position, the Japanese patrol ships and planes likely would have spotted them. They would have radioed back to Japan the position of the American ships, sending hundreds of planes to swarm down and destroy them. Most likely the B-25s would not have had a chance to take off. If they did, they would have been shot down quickly. This would have been a devastating blow to the United States. I believe that the sighting by the Japanese picket boat was no accident, because this was only the first of several unusual events that happened on this mission.

Having to take off in bad weather made it harder for the Japanese to spot the planes. The B-25s found clearer weather over Japan, which was needed to make their bombing run.

Another strange event was that an air raid drill was taking place when the planes arrived over Tokyo. This was the first time the Japanese planned an air raid drill, and it just happened to take place right at the very time that the bombers arrived. This helped the bombers a great deal.

The Japanese people thought Doolittle's planes were part of the drill. Once the bombers dropped their bombs, there was a lot of confusion. This helped the B-25s make their escape to China. Another thing that helped was the planes' insignia. At the beginning of the war, the United States insignia was a blue circle with an overlaid white star and a solid red circle in the middle of the star. The Japanese insignia is a big solid red circle. When the bombers flew over, the Japanese soldiers and pilots, seeing the red circle on the bombers, thought the planes were their own.

Once the Japanese realized that they were being bombed, they looked for Task Force 16. Here again, something remarkable worked out for the United States Navy. Doolittle's bombers did not have enough fuel to wait for all the planes to form a bomber formation, so each plane headed for Japan on its own.

When they arrived, the planes came in from different directions and at different times.

The Japanese had no idea as to which direction in which to look for the task force. Because all the planes began their flights over seven hundred miles from Japan, it took them three to four hours to reach their targets. By this time, the task force had turned around and was well on its way back to Pearl Harbor.

After turning toward China, the planes hit a head wind. This was a natural phenomenon. The wind at this time of year (April) always blew from China, across Japan, and all the way to the United States. (Note: we saw this happen in 2011, when an earthquake and tidal wave hit the coast of Japan. The nuclear power plant melted down, and radiation escaped. The wind was blowing it toward the United States. People in the United States were very afraid that the radiation would come over Hawaii and on to the West Coast.)

Here again, we see a very strange event take place. The wind shifted from a headwind to a tailwind just at the right time. This tailwind was a big help in getting the planes to China. Doolittle talked about this after the raid, saying, "And as we turned west across the Yellow Sea, the navigator said, 'I think we're going to have to ditch about two hundred miles (four hundred kilometers) off the coast, because we're getting pretty slim on the gas.' He called back about twenty minutes later and said, 'Good news! We've picked up a twenty-two-mile-an-hour (thirty-five-kilometer) tailwind, and this is the only reason on God's green earth the U.S. was able to get planes in over China.

We got about seventy miles (113 kilometers) inland before we had to bail out."

The wind changed from a headwind to a tailwind right when the planes needed it most. Very strange indeed … or was it? Or was Someone controlling the weather to help the bombers get to China? Just think about it!

Night was falling as the planes approached the coast of China; the weather got worse, and fuel was getting low. Not being able to see the ground or ocean, the pilots used their plane instruments to find Chengchow, approximately one hundred miles inland from the China coast. Of the sixteen planes in the bombing raid, eleven crews bailed out, four crash-landed or ditched off the Chinese coast, and one plane landed at Vladivostok in Russian Siberia. This crew was interned by the Russians for over a year.

Two fliers died in the crash landings, and one was killed after bailing out. Two of the crews were captured by the Japanese. Of the crew members that were captured, three men were executed by a Japanese firing squad on October 15, 1942. They were First Lieutenant William G. Farrow, First Lieutenant Dean Edward Hallmark, and Sergeant Harold A. Spatz. First Lieutenant Robert John Meder died on December 1, 1943, while a prisoner of the Japanese. The rest of the crews remained prisoners of war until the war's end. The crews of the other planes were picked up by Chinese peasants or guerrilla bands and taken to Chungking.

The Chinese paid dearly for helping the Americans. Chiang Kai-shek, the leader of China, was afraid of reprisals by the

Japanese because of the Americans' air raid. Soon after the raid, the Japanese forces wiped out entire villages, razed American and British church missions, and destroyed the airfields around Chengchow. It is estimated that 250,000 Chinese were killed, most of them civilians. Many of the Chinese did not even know that the Americans had bombed Japan. Chiang Kai-shek's fears of Japanese reprisals were realized.

Doolittle was still trying to locate some of his crews when he was ordered back to the United States on May 5. At first, Doolittle thought he was ordered back to be court-martialed. After all, he lost all of his planes, which were supposed to be turned over to the United States Army Air Corps in China. The planes were needed badly to fight the Japanese, and it was a great lost at this point in the war.

Much to his surprise, when he arrived back in the United States, he was not court-martialed but promoted to brigadier general. He was also summoned, with his wife, to the White House to receive the Congressional Medal of Honor (the highest US military medal) from President Roosevelt.

When the public heard about the raid on Japan, they and the press wanted to know from where the planes had come. When President Roosevelt was asked, he replied, "They came from our base in Shangri-La." Shangri-La was a mythical place of peace and joy where people live to be hundreds of years old. It was from a setting featured by James Hilton in his novel *Lost Horizon*. The book was very popular and was made into a motion picture in 1938. The Shangri-La remark by the president confounded the Japanese, for they too knew of the legend of Shangri-La.

The Doolittle raid was a great success for several reasons. First, it planted doubt in the minds of the Japanese people. They had been told that they would never be bombed. Yet just four months after the bombing of Pearl Harbor, the Japanese were attacked. Toshiko Matsumure was thirteen years old at the time of the air raid. Many years after the war, she was willing to tell her story.

She overheard the elders discussing it in hushed tones a few days after the raid. They were afraid the authorities would hear them. "It was a severe psychological shock, to even the most ardent believer, when it was officially announced that we had been attacked. We finally began to realize that all we were told was not true—that the government had lied when it said we were invulnerable. We then began to doubt that we were also not invincible."

It forced the Japanese to strengthen their home defenses, thus diverting resources that could have been used elsewhere. The raid gave the United States a morale boost. America needed an emotional shot in the arm, and some genuine heroes to look up to. The raid gave it to them. We now were able to strike back.

Perhaps most importantly, the raid forced the Japanese to rethink and reanalyze their military strategy in the Pacific. The military leaders had to save face and get back at the United States. They must destroy the United States aircraft carriers once and for all. The plan was to capture Midway Island and draw them out. It did not turn out that way.

The Japanese lost four of their largest aircraft carriers, many of their best pilots, and a great number of aircraft. The Battle of Midway became a major victory for the United States and was the turning point in the war in the Pacific. The Doolittle raid was the catalyst needed to start the United States on the road to victory in the Pacific. It was not a failure as Doolittle first thought.

Could all these strange things happening at just the right time have been a series of coincidences, or was Someone looking down and making them happen just when they were needed? It makes one wonder, doesn't it?

The Bible says that God controls the weather, and He changes kings' minds; He also takes down and builds up kingdoms. You can read this in the Bible. Here are some examples: Daniel 2:20–21, Jeremiah 18:7–8, Proverbs 21:1, and Mark 8:22.

10

Battle of the Coral Sea

After bombing Pearl Harbor, the Japanese moved into the Philippines, Gilbert Islands, Guam, New Britain, and Wake Island, picking more and more territory in the South Pacific.

Their next plan was to move farther south to Australia, New Zealand, and New Guinea, all US allies. The Japanese knew the United States would continue to support these countries. Japan needed a new base from which to bomb Australia and to block American convoys.

The plan was to attack Port Moresby in New Guinea. Once captured, Japan would have a base from which to operate in the southern Pacific. They would be able to bomb Australia, New Zealand, and American convoys coming to Australia. Their plan was to secure the port by May 10, 1942.

Up until then, the Japanese Imperial Navy and military troops had free reign of the Pacific, and all was going well for Japan. Once they captured Port Moresby, it would be very difficult for the Allies to regain the Pacific. Japan would have bases all around its homeland and be very secure in its territories. By doing this, the Japanese again hoped the United States would sue for peace and let them keep the territories they had captured.

On the other hand, if the United States did not sue for peace, then Japan planned to take Midway Island. This would give the Japanese a base to strike the Hawaiian Islands and perhaps even invade Hawaii and capture it. It would bring them that much closer to the US mainland.

The United States was able to break the Japanese communication code. They knew that Port Moresby would be attacked by the Japanese and that they had to send a task force there to stop them.

The plan called for taking the island of Tulagi on May 2, and Port Moresby on May 10, 1942. When Admiral Nimitz, commander of the naval forces in the South Pacific, learned of the Japanese invasion of Port Moresby, he ordered Task Force 17, which was already there, to find and destroy the Japanese. Task Force 17, under the command of Admiral Fletcher, had the aircraft carrier *Yorktown*, six destroyers, three cruisers, and two oilers. Admiral Nimitz also ordered Task Force 11, which was near New Caledonia, to head for Port Moresby. Task Force 11 was under the command of Admiral Fitch. He had the aircraft carrier *Lexington*, two cruisers, and five destroyers.

The Japanese divided their invasion forces into three groups. The first group, to invade the island of Tulagi, was made up of two mine layers, two destroyers, six minesweepers, two subcases, and a transport carrying four hundred troops. The second attack force, to attack Port Moresby, had eleven transport ships carrying five thousand soldiers, three light cruisers, a seaplane tender, three gunboats, and six destroyers. The first Japanese task force would invade Tulagi and then proceed to Port Moresby to help the task force there. These two task forces were protected by a third group carrier strike force with two aircraft carriers, two heavy cruisers, and six destroyers.

To protect the Japanese fleet from the Americans, four Japanese submarines formed a scouting line forty to fifty miles southwest of Guadalcanal. The submarines were to detect any Americans approaching and to warn the Japanese fleet. The decision to put the submarines on patrol in that location came too late, as the American task forces had already passed through, and the Japanese submarines never found the American fleet.

I do not believe this was by chance. I believe the decision being made too late was part of God's plan so that the American forces would be ready to repel the Japanese. American Task Force 17 and Task Force 11 united near New Caledonia on May 1. The two task forces began refueling. Task Force 17 refueled from the tanker USS *Neosho*, and then continued on to Port Moresby. Task Force 11 did not finish refueling until the next day and was then ordered to join up with Task Force 44 from Australia. General Douglas MacArthur was in command in Australia and sent this task force out to help in the battle of Tulagi and Port Moresby. Task Force 44 was made up of three cruisers and three destroyers.

On May 3, the Japanese task force landed on Tulagi. The small Australian commando unit and reconnaissance units evacuated before the Japanese arrived. Upon hearing that the Japanese task force had taken over the island of Tulagi, Task Force 17, with the aircraft carrier *Yorktown*, arrived on May 4 and sent its aircraft against the Japanese on the island. The Japanese had no warning that the Americans were coming because their submarines had arrived at their stations too late.

The Americans were able to sink a Japanese destroyer and three minesweepers, and damage four other ships. They also destroyed four seaplanes that were supporting the Japanese landings. The Americans lost only one dive bomber and two fighter planes, but the crews were picked up from the sea. When the Japanese heard of the Americans attacking their troops on Tulagi, they thought that the American task force was near the Solomon Islands. They headed there and found no Americans at all. Why the Japanese headed for the Solomon Islands is unknown. I believe God confused them so that the Americans could escape unharmed. On May 5, Task Forces 11, 17, and 44 joined and proceeded to look for the Japanese invasion forces. On May 6, Japanese scout planes spotted the American task force and notified their headquarters. The Japanese forces were three hundred miles away from the American ships and were refueling, so they could not go after the Americans. Also, for some reason, there was a low-hanging overcast of clouds above the American fleet, which made it difficult for the Japanese planes to find them.

It is quite a coincidence that it was overcast above the American fleet so the Japanese could not find it, don't you think? Meanwhile, an American B-17, based in Australia, spotted the

Japanese Port Moresby invasion force. The plane (although it was alone) attacked the task force, and the pilot radioed back to Australia telling what he saw. Another strange thing that happened was that the Japanese invasion force attacked Port Moresby several times during the day on May 6 without much success. You would think they would have had great success, considering all the ships they had.

Back in Australia, General MacArthur's headquarters radioed to the American task force the Japanese location, sending them in that direction as fast they could. On May 7, things began to get very confusing. The Japanese and the Americans sent out scout planes in all different directions looking for each other. Neither one could find the other until about seven thirty in the morning. One of the Japanese scout planes said he found an American carrier, a cruiser, and three destroyers. Another quickly said the same thing.

The Japanese sent all their planes out thinking they had spotted an American carrier, but it was not an American carrier. It was the oil tanker USS *Neosho* and its escort ship USS *Sims*. When the planes arrived with a total of seventy-eight aircraft, they found no Americans except the oil tanker; so, in desperation they attacked. Finally, at about 8:30 a.m., another Japanese plane found the American carriers and immediately reported what he saw.

Now, more confusion occurred, because all the planes were sent after the USS *Neosho*. The Japanese did not know what to do and began to think the American carriers had split up. What is interesting is that these were the same pilots that attacked

Pearl Harbor. At that time, the pilots had no problem seeing that the USS *Neosho* was a tanker. So how did they think it was an aircraft carrier this time? I am sure that God confused the pilots so the Japanese would send their planes after the wrong ships. Despite their success in sinking the USS *Sims* and USS *Neosho*, their mistake cost the Japanese a lot of aircraft because some of them never returned to their carriers. Some were shot down, and others ran out of fuel. This was a great blow to lose so many airplanes and pilots so soon in the battle.

On the American side, there was just as much confusion, with their forces believing that an American plane had spotted the Japanese. A B-17 spotted a Japanese task force, so they quickly sent their planes in that direction. From the information they received from the USS *Sims*, USS *Neosho*, and the B-17, the American pilots from aircraft carrier USS *Lexington* were able to find one of the Japanese carriers. They immediately dropped two one-thousand-pound bombs and five torpedoes and hit it. More airplanes followed from USS *Yorktown* to finish the job by scoring more hits on the carrier, sinking it. The Japanese task force then withdrew to safer waters. American airplanes returned to their carriers to rearm and refuel, but the day was drawing to a close. Admiral Fletcher decided to hold off another strike until the next day. The aircraft carriers stayed concealed from Japanese spotter planes under a very thick overcast.

All throughout the battle, there were overcast skies and squalls in the area that caused a lot of confusion. Also, both sides picked up each other's radio traffic, causing even more confusion. The Japanese launched aircraft because they believed that there was a sighting of the American aircraft carriers. As they went out, they were spotted by American fighters, who attacked and shot down seventy of their planes. The Japanese planes had no warning because the American planes came out of the overcast.

More confusion ensued when some of the Japanese planes managed to escape. Seeing some carriers up ahead, they assumed they were Japanese and prepared to land. In reality they were the American carriers, but in the darkness they couldn't tell and began their landing approach. Once the Japanese pilots realized that these were American carriers, they had to escape as quickly as possible before they were shot down. Even the Americans were so shocked that they didn't fire a shot at the Japanese planes.

The squalls then moved over the Japanese ships, which limited the visibility for both sides, and also hid the Japanese from the American search planes. One of the search pilots from the USS *Lexington* spotted the Japanese carriers through a hole in the clouds. This hole just happened to be right above the Japanese ships. At the same time, the Japanese planes spotted the Americans, so both sides launched attacks on each other. The American planes hit the second carrier with two one-thousand-pound bombs and five torpedoes, tearing open the front end of the ship. The attack caused heavy damage to the second carrier's flight and hangar decks. Aircraft from USS *Lexington* arrived and hit the same carrier with a one-thousand-pound bomb and two torpedoes, causing structural damage. With the flight deck damaged, loss of most of their aircraft, and many wounded, the last Japanese carrier was unable to conduct further operations and withdrew. The rest of the aircraft from the American carriers were unable to find the Japanese because of the heavy clouds.

Aircraft from the Japanese carriers were in the air at the time of the American attack and found the *Lexington* and the *Yorktown*. Two Japanese torpedoes hit the *Yorktown*. One torpedo hit the aviation gas storage tanks underneath the flight deck of the *Lexington*. Another torpedo plane attacked and hit the ship again, damaging the boiler. More Japanese planes came in and attacked the *Lexington* and the *Yorktown*, with dive bombers damaging both ships.

With heavy losses on both sides, the American carriers withdrew to repair their damaged ships. The Japanese radioed they were unable to fight because they had no air cover for the invasion force. Orders came in from Japan to withdraw. The aircraft carrier *Lexington* was so badly damaged that they had to abandon the ship. An American destroyer fired five torpedoes at the burning ship and sank it. The *Yorktown* was ordered back to Pearl Harbor as soon as possible for repairs to get ready for the next battle. Years later, in 1972, Vice Admiral Ductwork, after reading Japanese records of the battle, said, "Without a doubt, May 7, 1942, in the Coral Sea was the most confused battle in world history." I believe God let this confusion continue to cause the Japanese very poor luck and save much of the American fleet.

The Battle of the Coral Sea was not the biggest battle fought in World War II. However, it was the first time two enemy fleets never really saw each other and were fighting only by using each other's aircraft. The results of the Battle of the Coral Sea caused the Japanese to lose one aircraft carrier and damaged the second so that it could not participate in the upcoming Battle of Midway. The Japanese also lost a lot of trained pilots and aircraft, and they would be sorely missed in upcoming Pacific battles. A destroyer and several smaller ships were also lost. The American losses were a carrier, an oiler, and a destroyer.

It was good for the Americans and the Allies that Port Moresby was never invaded and captured by the Japanese. The southern route to Australia was left open, allowing the Americans to continue supplying to the Australians. It also stopped the Japanese from putting a base at Port Moresby to use in attacking Australia. It was a great tactical blow, and the first time the Japanese were pushed back. However, it certainly was not the last.

I believe God had a hand in this battle by keeping the Japanese from taking Port Moresby in New Guinea. This, of course, was a great achievement. It lifted the morale of the Allied forces in the Pacific, and began to turn the tide in their favor. It also prepared the way for the Battle of Midway. I believe God definitely had His hand in this battle. He changed the weather and caused a lot of confusion, stopping the Japanese from taking Port Moresby. If they had, it would have cut off the South Pacific from the rest of the world. Maybe the Japanese would have even captured Australia and New Zealand. This would have made the war last a lot longer and made it harder for the Allies to win.

11

Battle of Midway

As the Battle of the Coral Sea was going on, Admiral Yamamoto, who was the head of the Japanese combined fleet, was looking at the next South Pacific operation. He wanted to take the island of Midway. Midway Island is exactly that, an island midway between Japan and the islands of Hawaii. If the Japanese took the island, they would have a very forward base to protect the Pacific territories and to launch more strikes against the Hawaiian Islands. They could put in a naval base and utilize the island's airstrip for their bombers. Their goal was to destroy the remaining US aircraft carriers at Midway Island, hoping that the United States would be willing to negotiate a peace treaty and let Japan keep the territory it had captured. After the Japanese loss in the Coral Sea, it became even more important for them to take Midway in order to regain a strategic advantage.

Even with the loss of one aircraft carrier and another severely damaged in the Battle of the Coral Sea, Admiral Yamamoto still believed Japan had the upper hand in the number of aircraft carriers operating in the Pacific. From the incorrect information he had received, the United States had lost two of its carriers in the Coral Sea, leaving them with only two carriers operating, while Japan had at least four operational aircraft carriers.

About the same time, the United States broke the Japanese secret code and discovered that they were going to invade the island of Midway. The Battle of Midway took place June 3–7, 1942, only six months after Pearl Harbor and a month after the Battle of the Coral Sea. Admiral Chester Nimitz was commander of the US naval fleet. Even though he had fewer ships than the Japanese, he knew he had to stop them at Midway Island or the United States West Coast and the Hawaiian Islands would be in great danger.

Meanwhile, the USS *Yorktown* limped back to Pearl Harbor, and immediately the navy shipyard began repairing it. If the Japanese had destroyed the Pearl Harbor repair yards on December 7, the USS *Yorktown* would have gone to San Francisco or San Diego for repairs. This would have kept the *Yorktown* from the Battle of Midway. However, by not destroying the repair yards, the US Navy was able to repair most of its ships that were damaged or sunk in the attack. This was one of the major blunders of the Japanese attack on Pearl Harbor.

I believe that God knows the future and prevented those repair yards from being destroyed. The navy was then able to get its ships back in fighting condition at Pearl Harbor, rather than go to San Francisco or San Diego. When the USS *Yorktown* arrived, workers were waiting for it and began repairs immediately. It only took three days and nights to get USS *Yorktown* back in fighting condition and on its way to Midway Island. Normally, it would have taken weeks, maybe even months, to get the ship back in fighting condition. This is another example of God's hand in history.

The United States had one more carrier, the USS *Saratoga*. It was on the West Coast undergoing repairs, but it was not ready to sail and join the fleet leaving from Pearl Harbor. The USS *Yorktown* lost much of its aircraft in the Battle of the Coral Sea. New air crews and aircraft from the USS *Saratoga* were transferred to the Yorktown. Without the USS *Yorktown*, there would have been only two American aircraft carriers at the Battle of Midway, the USS *Enterprise* and the USS *Hornet*. If the Americans had one less aircraft carrier, the Japanese would have outnumbered them by two to one.

On Midway Island, the United States had aircraft from both the army and the Marine Corps. The United States Marines had many antiaircraft guns and long-range artillery for use against any naval ship that came close to the island. Although many of these aircraft were obsolete at the time, the planes and pilots distinguished themselves in this battle. They were a distraction to the Japanese fleet, and this distraction helped US carriers find them. These men made a great sacrifice, which helped win the Battle of Midway.

Another factor contributing to the Japanese loss at Midway was the fact that their ships, planes, and crews had been out at sea since November 1941. The Japanese had at least four aircraft carriers available to them; however, two of them had been at sea so long that they needed repairs and maintenance. With so many aircraft carriers at their disposal, they should have rotated them. This way, their crews and ships would not have been in so much need of rest and repair. Again, I see God's hand in this situation.

Another factor that led to the Japanese loss was Admiral Yamamoto's hesitation in deploying submarines to look for the American fleet. Just as in the Battle of the Coral Sea, they put the submarines out at the wrong time and in the wrong place. Because of this, the submarines never did find the American aircraft carriers at Midway. The American aircraft carriers positioned themselves northeast of Midway, named "Point Luck," because they arrived before the Japanese submarines went on patrol to find them.

I don't believe that it was just luck. God's hand was involved in this as well. The Japanese radio operators intercepted numerous messages between American submarines. They did not inform Admiral Yamamoto or any other official about the radio traffic or even try to locate where the signals were coming from. It is still a mystery today why the Japanese navy never investigated the radio messages, or tried to locate the American submarines, which were probably near the US fleet. This mystery can be solved by looking to God.

At 9:00 a.m. on June 3, 1942, a US Navy patrol aircraft from Midway Island spotted the Japanese task force 580 miles away. The crew thought it was the main Japanese task force, but they were mistaken. It was a smaller group of ships joining up with the main Japanese task force. Nine B-17s and some navy planes took off from Midway Island to attack the group. They dropped their bombs but caused little damage. Admiral Nagumo, who was in charge of the attacking Japanese fleet, launched his initial attack on the island. Interestingly enough, Admiral Nagumo was the same admiral in charge of the Japanese fleet that attacked Pearl Harbor.

Early in the morning of June 4, both the Japanese and American aircraft went searching for each other's ships. As they were launching their planes to bomb Midway Island, the Americans found two Japanese aircraft carriers. Meanwhile, the Japanese search planes could not find the American fleet because of low overcast skies. It is interesting that the American fleet was again hidden by clouds, while the Japanese fleet had clear skies over them.

The American planes from Midway Island attacked the Japanese ships. With the Japanese fighter cover, most of the American planes were shot down and lost. However, they were able to warn the island that the Japanese were coming, and the marines on the island were prepared for the attack. The Japanese aircraft heavily damaged the US base on Midway but did not knock it out of action. The United States Marines shot down eleven aircraft, heavily damaged fourteen, and damaged twenty-nine more before the Japanese returned to their carriers. The Japanese still had quite a few aircraft left, and here's where things began to get very curious.

After returning to the carriers, the Japanese pilots said they were unable to knock out Midway's runway, so a second attack would have to be launched. During the counterattack by the Americans, a B-26 aircraft was shot down by the Japanese, and it crashed near Admiral Nagumo's ship. Seeing that American land-based bombers were still operating from Midway Island, Admiral Nagumo was convinced to launch the second attack on Midway. Here again, we see another of the many mistakes the Japanese made. Admiral Nagumo was so busy getting ready to bomb Midway Island, using every available aircraft, that he did not have the aircraft he needed to protect his fleet and to go after the American ships.

The standard procedure for naval operations of Japanese aircraft carriers was to only use half of the aircraft for attacking and keep the other half to defend against enemy ships or aircraft. At Midway Island, Admiral Nagumo ordered the second group of aircraft, supposedly reserved to protect against enemy attack, to rearm and drop bombs on the island.

Admiral Nagumo broke from the standard military tactics because he believed there were no American ships nearby. His scout planes did not report any enemy ships. This again is another mistake in which I believe God's hand was involved. As his planes were being rearmed, a message came in that a Japanese scout plane had spotted the American carriers. Now Admiral Nagumo didn't know what to do. A major part of the strike force that hit Midway Island was returning and needed to land immediately, because they were out of fuel, and some of them were damaged.

There was mass confusion on the aircraft carriers. The second group of planes, preparing to launch against the American ships, were being rearmed. They were removing the torpedoes and loading regular bombs to attack Midway. So, in all this confusion, bombs and torpedoes were on the flight deck and in the hangar bay below, instead of in the munitions storage compartment.

In the midst of all this, American planes from Midway Island attacked the fleet again. Although these planes caused very little damage, they did add to the confusion. Admiral Nagumo was even more convinced to drop bombs on Midway Island.

Meanwhile, American aircraft carriers launched their planes against the Japanese and were headed right for them. The American aircraft carriers were 180 miles from the Japanese fleet. The planes, from the carriers *Enterprise* and *Hornet*, were at the maximum range for their aircraft. It also took quite a while for the Americans to launch all their aircraft, which used up a lot of fuel. To save fuel, the aircraft did not circle to regroup. They took off for their target, so the squadrons were scattered. The Americans did this for a couple of reasons. One was to confuse the Japanese carriers by launching a variety of attacks over a long period, and the other was to save fuel.

Unfortunately, things didn't go as planned. As the Americans arrived, many of the planes were low on fuel. They had to ditch in the ocean or return to their carriers. Many of the torpedo bombers had no protection. Torpedo Squadron 8, from the aircraft carrier *Enterprise*, was the first to attack the enemy, but not one plane survived. In fact, only one pilot survived. His name was George H. Gay. The entire squadron was lost. As the American planes kept coming in, more and more were shot down, and the losses for the United States began to get heavy.

Despite all the American losses, the sacrifice of these pilots and their planes contributed heavily to the destruction of the Japanese fleet. The attack planes threw the Japanese off balance. The aircraft carriers had to maneuver to protect themselves from the torpedoes being dropped. This, of course, made it difficult to launch more planes or recover aircraft. The planes in the air, protecting the carriers, were getting low on ammunition and fuel. This became a major problem for the Japanese; they lost planes and their best pilots. This caused a very big disadvantage in fighting the Americans.

While the Japanese fighters protected the carriers, and focused on the torpedo planes, *Enterprise* and *Yorktown* dive bombers arrived on the scene. They came in from several different directions, throwing the Japanese off even more. Meanwhile, on the Japanese carriers' decks, planes sat with refueling hoses running from one aircraft to another. Bombs and torpedoes were also lying on the deck. They were now sitting ducks!

Two *Enterprise* squadrons split up, and each squadron attacked one of the carriers. The planes dove on the first carrier and made five direct hits, causing heavy damage and many fires. One bomb hit near the ship's bridge, killing the captain and many of its officers. A few minutes later, the other American squadron dove on another carrier. Only one bomb made a hit, but it hit the right spot. It penetrated the upper deck into the hangar. This contained a large number of bombs, torpedoes, and planes being refueled, which caused a great explosion. One of the Japanese on board said bodies were flying everywhere and flames were shooting up all over. It was impossible to bring the fire under control. Another bomb struck in the water and went off near the stern, damaging the rudder and causing the ship to go out of control.

Yorktown dive bombers scored three hits on the third aircraft carrier, causing extensive damage. Gasoline tanks were ignited. Fires broke out, spreading to the bombs and ammunition sitting on the decks. This caused more explosions, and the ship was going down. It did not take long before all three aircraft carriers were abandoned and began to sink.

The Japanese were not yet defeated. They still had one aircraft carrier and found USS *Yorktown* by following the American aircraft back to the carrier. The Japanese hit the *Yorktown* with three bombs that went through the flight and hangar decks before exploding down in the boilers. The crew got the fires under control and started some of the boilers, allowing the ship to get under way. One hour later, a second Japanese attack wave consisting of ten torpedo bombers and six fighters arrived over the *Yorktown*. They attacked and hit the ship with two torpedoes. This time, all power was lost. The ship was listing twenty-three degrees, but the Americans shot down five of the torpedo bombers and two fighters.

Later that afternoon, an *Enterprise* scout plane located the fourth Japanese aircraft carrier, and twenty-four dive bombers took off to attack it. The American attack aircraft were met by many Japanese fighters. The Americans scored at least four hits on the aircraft carrier and set it ablaze. After trying to put out the fires, the Japanese sailors abandoned ship. By the next morning, the fourth aircraft carrier had sunk.

On June 7, 1942, while the Americans were towing the USS

Yorktown to Hawaii, a Japanese submarine fired two torpedoes. The ship then began to sink. Because the ship was mostly abandoned, very few of its crew lost their lives. Most of the crew were able to get off and were rescued by a destroyer.

The American aircraft carriers pulled back and prepared for another attack, but the attack never came. The next day, the Japanese (with their cruisers and destroyers) continued looking for the American aircraft carriers. They still did not find them, because the Americans were too far away. During the next few days, the Japanese and the American forces had minor spotting of each other, but very little action took place for one reason or another. Several American air strikes sank one more Japanese cruiser, and another one was damaged before the Americans withdrew.

The Battle of Midway was over. The Japanese suffered heavy casualties in men, aircraft, and ships. The Americans lost one aircraft carrier, many airplanes, and men, but ultimately won the battle. The Battle of Midway was now the turning point in the war in the Pacific. Japan was unable to take any more territory and now was on the defensive. Although the war would last another three years, the United States saw that it was going to eventually win in the Pacific.

I believe all the things that took place in the Battle of Midway show us that God certainly was involved. He had to stop the Japanese from taking over in the Pacific, and He was the One who could turn the tide. As we read in the Bible: "The king's heart is in the hand of the Lord, Like the rivers of water; He turns it wherever He wishes" (Proverbs 21:19 NKJV). In the Battle of Midway, God caused Admiral Nagumo to keep changing his mind so that the Japanese fleet was in chaos.

As I have often said before, God never wanted war, but in his infinite wisdom, He could see what was going to happen if Japan and Germany were to win. God stepped in at the right time to stop them. As you can see, God and Satan used people to do their bidding. Eventually both Japan and Germany would surrender, but without God's help, the world could have been a very different place today.

12

June 6, 1944: D-Day

I n the spring of 1944, General Dwight D. Eisenhower, the Allied supreme commander in Europe, had to make one of the most important decisions of World War II. Hundreds of thousands of Allied soldiers, sailors, and airmen awaited his orders to begin Operation Overlord, also known as "D-Day," the invasion of France. General Eisenhower had already delayed Operation Overlord for a month. He postponed other military operations to allow the Allies enough time to build up troops and gather together the needed ships and landing craft. He set the date for June 5, 1944.

The Allied planners knew they could not control the weather for D-Day. Late on the evening of June 2, 1944, General Eisenhower, his top generals, and British Prime Minister Winston Churchill met to review the weather forecast. The news was not good. D-Day, June 5, promised cloudy skies, rain, and heavy seas. General Eisenhower chose to wait one more day to see if the weather forecast might improve. Less than twenty-four hours before the scheduled invasion, General Eisenhower gathered his advisers again. The forecast indicated that the rain would stop, and there would be a break in the clouds by midafternoon on June 6. Eisenhower decided to give the go-ahead for D-Day on June 6. This was a surprise. Everyone believed the weather would not change for another week.

The D-Day operation of June 6, 1944, brought together the land, air, and sea forces of the Allied armies, in what became known as the largest invasion force in human history. The operation, given the code name Overlord, delivered five naval assault divisions to the beaches of Normandy, France. The beaches were given the code names Utah, Omaha, Gold, Juno, and Sword. A great invasion force stood off the coast of Normandy as dawn broke on June 6: nine battleships, twenty-three cruisers, 104 destroyers, and seventy-one large landing craft of various descriptions carrying tanks and trucks. They also carried hundreds of troop transports and mine sweepers. This was the largest naval armada ever assembled. It included seven thousand ships and landing craft manned by over 195,000 naval personnel from eight Allied countries. Almost 133,000 troops from England, Canada, and the United States landed on D-Day. Casualties from the three countries during the invasion numbered 10,300. By June 30, over 850,000 men, 148,000 vehicles, and 570,000 tons of supplies had landed on the Normandy coast. The naval bombardment began at 5:50 a.m., detonating large minefields along the shoreline. This lasted for about one hour.

Field Marshal Von Rundstedt was in charge of the German defense of France. He was a nobleman from the German province known as Prussia, and he was also a World War I general.

He did not like Hitler and would not talk to him if he could avoid it. Hitler was merely a corporal in World War I and was just a peasant, not a nobleman.

When the invasion force landed, Field Marshal Von Rundstedt had his second in command ask Hitler for the two reserved tank divisions to push back the Allies. Hitler had taken a sleeping pill, and no one at his headquarters dared to awaken him. Hitler, in his tirades, had been known to order executions of his people. Reporting back to Von Rundstedt, his second told him to ask Hitler himself because he was the head of France's defenses, and Hitler should listen to him. However, Von Rundstedt said that he would not go crawling to that little corporal.

At that same time, Field Marshal Erwin Rommel (known as the "Desert Fox" and a former commander in World War I) was in charge of the Normandy defense. Coincidently, he was back in Germany for his wife's birthday, which happened to be on June 6.

Because of the bad weather, many of the top German generals were away participating in war games. Many thought it would be a good time to take an extra day for a holiday, and left a day early on June 5, since the weather was not supposed to get better for another week. This left only lower-ranking officers in charge, who had little power to move troops.

In the US and British armies, lower-ranking officers can make decisions on the movement of their troops as needed, based on what is happening at the time. If there was an American tank division, the general in charge could see what was going on and had authority to move the tanks. In the German and Japanese military, lower-ranking officers could not make such decisions. They did not have the power to move their tanks into the fight, which allowed the Allies to take the beaches.

While the Germans were putting their faith in the weather forecast, General Eisenhower, who was monitoring the weather closely, decided to take advantage of the one day of good weather and ordered the invasion of Normandy. Here is another one of the things that showed me that God was involved.

Was it just a coincidence that Rommel was back in Germany for his wife's birthday? And that her birthday fell on the only day the weather cleared? If the weather had cleared sooner, Rommel would not have left France and would have conducted the counterattack. Also, he may have convinced Hitler to give him the two German tank divisions, which could have stopped the Allies' landings. Many of the other German generals were not with their troops. Instead, they were meeting on how to stop the Allied invasion. By the time they returned to the front, it was too late.

I believe all this was not just bad luck. There were too many things happening all at the same time for it to be just a coincidence. Hitler had to be stopped. If the world had been left to him, there would be no freedom for anyone. Hitler would not have stopped with taking over Europe; he wanted to control the world. I believe God was very much involved and helped the Allies on D-Day. I'll leave it up to you to decide for yourself, but the Bible says God promises to help us. "With God's help we will do well. And He will break under His feet those who fight against us" (Psalm 60:12 NKJV).

13

Battle of the Bulge

By December 1944, the Allies had pushed the Germans from France and Belgium almost to the border of Germany. They moved so fast that the supply lines could not keep up because there were not sufficient deep water ports left intact. The advance had to stop at the German border to wait for men and supplies. The weather had turned cold, as it was now winter, so the Allied troops could rest and wait for spring before moving into Germany.

The Allies believed the war would be over soon, because all that was left was to take Germany. The intelligence reports coming in were saying that the Germans had little fight left in them. They also stated that the German army was completely destroyed, the air force was no more, and their navy had been sunk. All that was left was to move across the Rhine River from the west, as the Russians would be moving in from the east. They thought it would only be a matter of days before the Germans surrendered; however, Germany was not finished yet.

Germany still had a lot of men, mostly very old and very

young, but they were willing to fight. The Allies had not destroyed the German industries. They were still producing the V1 and the V2 rockets, which were being fired at London. Also, the Germans were building a new and better tank called the King Tiger Two. This type was far superior to any tank that the Allies had.

Things did not look very good, with the Allies ready to advance from the west, and the Russians soon to cross the border in the east. This forced the Nazi army to retreat back to Germany, all across both fronts. However, Hitler believed his back was up against the wall.

Hitler knew he could not make a peace treaty with the Russians. He did, however, think he could make one with the British and the Americans, if he could split their forces and capture the Port of Antwerp. He was trying to prove that his army was still strong, and the war would keep going for a long time. If he could make a peace treaty with the Allies, he could then turn his full force against the Russians. This would give him more time to develop his new superweapons.

His plan was to launch an attack in the Ardennes in Belgium, the weakest part of the Allies' front line. Because the forest was very thick with trees and brush, it was hard to see anything hidden from the air or the ground. This was not the first time that the Germans had attacked through the Ardennes.

In World War I, the German army attacked Belgium through the Ardennes, pushing the Allies back into France. In the 1940 Battle of France, the German army did it again. They came right through the Ardennes and, in just a few months, were all the way to the French coast. There was no stopping them that time. So, if it worked twice before, why not do it a third time?

The Germans brought up 450,000 men, over twelve hundred tanks, and over forty-two hundred pieces of artillery. The Allies did not know that the Germans had that many forces left. The Germans brought these forces in over many nights and hid them for weeks. The attack began on December 16, 1944. The Americans along the line were outnumbered and taken by surprise. The first few days all went well for the Germans, as they were able to push deep into the Allies' line. In fact, they caused a bulge in the line seventy miles wide and fifty miles deep. This is why it is called the Battle of the Bulge.

Hitler's tank divisions moved so quickly that the Americans were totally unprepared. The Germans encircled the American troops near the city of St. Vith, capturing about two-thirds of the 106th Infantry Division. General Bradley moved reinforcements into the town, preventing the Germans from capturing it completely. Throughout the Battle of the Bulge, the weather limited the Allies' ability to use their air support. Even though the Allies were able to slow the advance, the Germans captured many American soldiers. One of the German divisions belonged to the SS. (Hitler's elite and fanatical troops). During the battle, this German division captured a number of American soldiers, lined them up against the wall and machine-gunned them down. When the Allies heard about this atrocity, there would be no more thought of surrender.

Another German tank division surrounded the town of Bastogne. The American 101st Airborne Division was in the town and fought hard, stopping the German advance. Once the Germans had completely surrounded the town, they commanded the Americans to surrender. General Anthony McAuliffe replied to the Germans with one word: "Nuts."

General Bradley, commander of all American forces in France, gave General Patton permission to take three divisions from his Third Army to rescue and relieve the 101st Airborne Division in Bastogne. When General Patton heard what General McAuliffe said to the Germans, Patton said, "We have to save that magnificent blankety-blank," and he laughed, but he did not say "blankety-blank."

As I said before, the weather was a major problem for the Allies in getting air support. General Patton believed there was only one way to get the weather to cooperate, so he ordered his chaplain to give him a prayer that would clear the weather. The chaplain, of course, was not sure how God would react to this prayer since he was asking God to clear the weather so they could kill the Germans. General Patton told the chaplain, "I want that prayer now. We need God on our side, or those soldiers in Bastogne will all die." Here is the famous prayer that General Patton's chaplain gave him:

"Almighty and most merciful Father, we humbly beseech Thee, of Thy great goodness, to restrain these immoderate rains with which we have had to contend. Grant us fair weather for battle. Graciously hearken to us as soldiers who call upon Thee that, armed with Thy power, we may advance from victory to victory, and crush the oppression and wickedness of our enemies and establish Thy justice among men and nations."

The next day, December 23, the weather cleared. In fact, it was perfect weather for six days. General Patton was so pleased with his chaplain that he gave him a medal, and said, "This man stands in good with the Lord."

So the Allied air forces attacked the German army and supplied the 101st Airborne Division in Bastogne. Without the food, ammunition, and medical supplies, they would not have lasted much longer. This was definitely a miracle for the Allied forces. Not only did they save the men in Bastogne, but they pushed back the entire German army.

The fighting continued through January 25, 1945, but the Germans were on the run back to Germany. The Battle of the Bulge was over with a major victory for the Allies. The casualties were very high. The United States had seventy-five thousand casualties, the greatest number of casualties ever suffered in a single battle. The Germans suffered close to eighty-two thousand casualties.

The war was not yet over, as the fighting continued until May 1945. From now on, though, the fighting would be in Germany itself. With the Russians coming in from the east, and the British and the Americans from the west, they slowly encircled Berlin. The end was definitely in sight. Because the Russians had suffered so much from the hands of the Germans in Russia, General Eisenhower allowed the Russians to take Berlin. On May 2, 1945, the Germans surrendered, and the war in Europe was over.

There is no doubt that God intervened in the Battle of the Bulge. General Patton prayed for God's help for clear weather, and overnight the weather cleared, so the Allies were able to get air power and push back the German army.

14

The Atomic Bomb and the End of World War II

While American forces were fighting in Western Europe and in the Pacific, back at home a secret project was forming, the Manhattan Project. It was the development of the atomic bomb. It started many years before, when scientists discovered the atom. Then things really began to heat up in Germany in 1938, when two chemists were able to split the atom. They wrote a paper that was published in the scientific journals of the time. Because Germany was controlled by the Nazi Party in 1938, it became a very great concern to the scientists outside of Germany. One of these scientists was Albert Einstein. After reading the paper, he contacted the two German scientists. Einstein and several other US scientists worried the Germans would apply this technology and knowledge to the building of the atomic bomb. They wrote President Franklin Roosevelt a letter telling him about their concerns, stating that if the Germans built this weapon, they would no doubt use it against England and the United States.

When President Roosevelt received the letter, he immediately contacted General Marshall, who was in charge of the US military forces. When Marshall read the letter, he also became very concerned, even though America was not at war with Germany. Everyone knew it was only a matter of time before war would break out between the United States and Germany, and if this weapon existed, the Germans could control the world. President Roosevelt decided that if anybody was going to get this weapon first, it had to be the United States.

So President Roosevelt began the Manhattan Project. Manhattan, of course, was a city in New York State, and it was a very innocent idea to be name after a city. The project began slowly at first because very little money was given to the project. As time went on, however, more money, scientists, and laboratories around the country were designated for the project. By 1944, up to 129,000 people in twenty different places were working on the project. The most well-known places were Oak Ridge National Laboratories and Los Alamosa Proving Grounds.

Spies from all over the world wanted to know what the United States was doing. Even though it was very hush-hush, it's hard to keep a lid on a project when you have 129,000 people working in twenty different places. The Russians were the biggest concern, who succeeded in having inside spies working on the project. The Russians knew all about what was going on in the United States and were getting information on how to build an atomic bomb.

It took some time to begin developing the bomb in earnest. In 1945 Robert Oppenheimer, who was in charge of the Los

Alamos scientists, needed to test the weapon. The location he picked was Socorro, New Mexico (now called White Sands Proving Grounds). On July 16, 1945, they set off the first atomic bomb in the history of mankind. However, no one really knew exactly what was going to happen. Some scientists were afraid it would start a chain reaction and destroy the entire planet. Although it did start a chain reaction, it was short-lived, so the planet was spared.

At the same time, Germany was also experimenting with a bomb design of its own. Hitler thought it was unachievable, and chose not to put a lot of money into it. He did not believe in it, like he did not believe in the rocket or the jet plane. He was having enough trouble manufacturing the conventional weapons. By 1944 the Allied armies were moving into Germany. Money and resources were dwindling.

This, of course, was unknown to the Allies, so they continued working on the atomic bomb. In May 1945, Germany surrendered, and the war in Europe ended. The focus of the war shifted to defeating Japan in the Pacific. The Allied armies were winning many battles in the Pacific. Some of the most famous were Iwo Jima, Guadalcanal, and Okinawa. Over time, the Allies learned how fiercely the Japanese army, navy, and air force fought. They would rather die than surrender. In all those battles, very few Japanese soldiers, sailors, or airmen surrendered.

It became apparent that soon the Americans and their Allies needed to invade the country of Japan itself to end the war. Fighting in Japan would be even fiercer than the fighting in the other places in the Pacific Ocean. The Japanese would be fighting for their own country. Rumors were spreading, which were later found to be true, that the Japanese were teaching children to carry hand grenades, run into the midst of soldiers, and set the grenades off. They taught children, women, and the elderly to use five- to ten-foot-long sharp bamboo poles to impale soldiers. The only way the soldiers could survive this tactic would be to kill these people, which was very upsetting to American soldiers.

I once knew a man who attended my church. His name was Wayne McGregor. He fought in the Pacific for four years. He saw the Japanese soldiers and knew how hard it was to defeat them. He and the other American soldiers, sailors, marines, and airmen, who were preparing to invade Japan, felt that they were going to die. They even wrote their last wills and testaments and mailed them to their families back home. The American soldiers knew what had to be done to win this war and were willing to make the ultimate sacrifice.

Back in Washington, President Roosevelt looked at the cost to defeat the Japanese on Japanese soil. The military estimated that the United States would suffer one million casualties. Judging from the way the Japanese soldiers fought in the Pacific, it was certain that they would fight even harder defending their homeland. No doubt, Japanese casualties would be many times greater. Some estimates ran as high as ten million.

Of course, the American military and its citizens did not know the United States was building the atomic bomb. Even Vice President Harry Truman did not know about the atomic bomb. When Truman was a senator, he was on a committee investigating abuse of private companies' contracts to build military equipment for the US armed forces. While he was investigating many of these allegations and problems, he came across a program called the Manhattan Project. It was costing the government millions, and he had no idea what it was. He and his staff began to look into it.

One day while he was working, he received a call from the president to come the White House immediately. When Senator Truman arrived at the president's office, he saw President Roosevelt sitting at his desk, and standing next to him was General Marshall, chief of staff of all the US military. Truman was told that he and his staff were to drop any investigation of the Manhattan Project. They told him it was vital that he comply. It was not until he became president that he was told about the Manhattan Project.

President Truman was told that the atomic bomb tests were successful in Nevada. When the war got closer to Japan, he had to make a decision. Should he use the bomb or send American military personnel to invade Japan? Harry Truman had fought in World War I and knew the cost of war. He had commanded an artillery battery that endured shelling back-and-forth between them and the Germans. When the time came, President Truman believed he had no choice but to use the atomic bomb on Japan.

Over the years, many people have said that he should not have done this. I believe that his background and understanding of war (having participated in war himself) gave him the knowledge to see that he had to use the bomb. I also believe that God, in His infinite wisdom, knew that this war would go on for at least one or maybe two more years, and the death toll would rise dramatically after the Americans landed on Japanese soil. This bloodshed had to come to an end. By dropping the two bombs, close to two hundred thousand people died, and many more died later from radiation sickness. This was horrible, but there was much less bloodshed than if Allied soldiers had landed in the country itself. Literally, millions of Americans and Japanese would have been killed.

Did Harry Truman do the right thing? People are still debating about that to this day. It's important to understand how World War II was handled. Bombing cities was part of the war. It all started back on December 13, 1937, when Japanese planes bombed the city of Nanking in China. After that, Japanese soldiers came in and killed over two hundred thousand Chinese people. Now let us look at what was happening in the war in Europe. From the summer of 1940 until the end of World War II, Germany bombed London and other English cities. They called this the blitz (short for blitzkrieg) meaning "lightning war." Many thousands of people in England were killed. Now let us look at the United States and England.

The Royal Air Force and the US planes bombed many German cities, killing thousands of people, and continued to the end of the war. One of the most devastating US and British bombing campaigns conducted was the bombing of the city of Dresden, Germany. Over twelve hundred Royal Air Force and US Air Force bombers dropped thirty-nine hundred tons of high explosive and incendiary bombs on the city, causing a firestorm that destroyed the heart of the city and killed over twenty-three thousand citizens.

Finally, let us look at what was happening in Russia when Germany invaded. Moscow and many cities were bombed by the Germans. One city in particular was Leningrad, where a great battle ensued. The city was literally laid to waste, and many thousands of Russian citizens were killed as well. Then, of course, there was US bombing of Japan from November 1944 to August 1945. The United States dropped tons of bombs and incendiaries, hitting Japanese cities. In Tokyo alone, over one hundred thousand people were killed from US bombs.

So what Harry Truman did was not unusual for that time. What was unusual was that he only needed one bomb to destroy a complete city. I believe that God placed Harry Truman in the White House after President Roosevelt died, because Truman knew what the cost would be if the war continued. I believe that President Roosevelt would have used the bomb to end this bloodshed as well. Remember, the war had gone on for many years already, and everyone was tired of the death toll.

War is not something that God wanted. Satan invented war, and it is all a part of sin. God stepped in to put a stop to it. God allowed the American forces to use the bombs on Japan to stop the bloodshed.

It has been many years since the United States dropped the bombs on Japan. Since then, by the help of God, no country has used the atomic bomb. The new hydrogen bomb, which has greater explosive power than the bombs dropped on Japan in 1945, has not been used either.

15

Aftermath

In 1945, World War II, the bloodiest and costliest war in the history of mankind, ended. The shooting war had stopped, but a new kind of war now started. They called it "the Cold War." When the German army took over all of Western Europe, they collected all the finest and most precious pieces of Western European art. They collected paintings of the masters (such as Gauguin, Ramallah, Pacosto), and sculptures from personal collectors and museums (such as the Louvre in Paris).

President Harry Truman requested that art experts and museum curators go to Europe to reclaim all that was stolen by the Germans. These men found many of the artworks and treasures that the Germans had stolen, but, unfortunately, some of these artworks were destroyed—many famous and priceless art pieces that could never be replaced.

At the same time, another US-British operation was called "Operation Paperclip." This operation was to capture German scientists and engineers that created such advanced weaponry as the world had never seen, and bring them to the United States and Great Britain. Some of these weapons were the V1 buzz bomb, the V2 ballistic missile, and the jet plane. Fortunately for the Allies, many of the scientists, such as Dr. Von Braun, wanted to come to the United States. He could continue working on his rockets, which would someday take man to the moon. Another famous engineer, who invented the jet engine, Hans Von Ohain, turned himself over (as did Dr. Von Braun) to the US Army. The US Army picked up as many of the V2 rockets and the new German jet fighter planes as they could. The Russians wanted these men, rockets, and planes as badly as the United States did. There was always a lot of distrust between the East and the West, but now it was becoming even greater.

The Russians took Berlin and wanted to keep it, along with the rest of Germany. Through a great deal of negotiation, a plan was drawn up to divide Germany and Berlin. The country of Germany was divided in half. The east side went to the Russians, and the west side went to France, Great Britain, and United States. The city of Berlin was divided the same way. As tensions grew, a wall was built through the center of Berlin. For many decades, it was called the Berlin Wall. It divided the city of Berlin in half, keeping the people in East Germany from escaping to West Germany. No wall was needed to stop people from going to East Germany.

The Cold War lasted until 1991, when the Berlin Wall came down, and the people of Germany united themselves. In the Soviet Union, as more and more time went by, the satellite nations broke away and created their own free countries. Several times during the Cold War, things began to heat up.

One of the events was the 1962 Cuban Missile Crisis. Russia was putting ballistic missiles with nuclear warheads on them in Cuba, where they could strike anywhere in the United States and South America. For a time, about two weeks, it looked like World War III was going to start. If it had, this war would have been fought with nuclear weapons, and the world would have been destroyed.

I believe God stepped in and convinced these men to stop their threats and talk peace. Remember the Bible verse that I quoted before: "The King's heart is in the hand of the Lord, like the rivers of water; He turns it wherever He wishes" (Proverbs 21:19 NKJV).

But wars continue today. We are now fighting a new kind, a war on terror. I believe we must trust in God to see us through the danger we are facing. God has seen the United States through World War II and many other wars. If we put our trust in Him, He will also see us through this present danger. In the Bible, He tells us He will take care of us and watch over us if we turn our lives over to Him. We have nothing to fear from the world.

Through this book, I hope you have seen how God has worked throughout the times of war. God never intended for us to be fighting in wars but wanted mankind to live in the garden of Eden in peace and happiness. He wanted to be there with them to help them make decisions. Yet mankind chose to follow Satan, not God. Mankind disobeyed God, and the consequences of that disobedience have been evident to us ever since.

Even though we brought this all upon ourselves, He never leaves us all alone. He is always there with his hand outstretched, wanting us to come back to Him. I hope this book has helped you see how God did not forsake us. Have you ever wondered if there is a God because of all the suffering you see in the world? He has to let sin play out. Through the great controversy between good and evil, you and I can see how evil Satan is. We can see what sin does to all of us and to this world that God created. Some people ask, "If God did not create evil, then how did it come about?" The Bible has the answer.

May God bless you and be with you. My prayer is that this book helped you see that there is a God. He does care for all of us, and someday He is coming back to take us home.

Glossary

blitzkrieg—Also known as the blitz. A German word for fast-moving attacks.

Bomber Command—What the British call the part of the RAF that oversaw the bombers.

bombardier—The crewman on the plane whose job it was to drop the bombs.

bombsight—Sighting device for aiming bombs.

B-17 and B-24—US heavy bombers.

B-25—Medium bomber.

chancellor—Prime Minister of Germany.

commanded—Have authority over.

D-Day—Code word for the Normandy invasion of France, June 1944.

Fighter Command—What the British called the part of the RAF that oversaw the fighter planes.

fuehrer—Supreme leader.

gauge—Size of railroad tracks.

Great Britain—Title for England, Ireland, Scotland, and other British territories.

hawks—People who were interested in the war in Europe and wanted to help England.

High Command—These are the generals and admirals in command of the military of their country. Like the Joint Chiefs of Staff in the US military.

Hurricane—British fighter plane.

incendiary bombs—Small stick-like bombs packed with fuel that burn and cause fires when they hit an object.

infrastructure—Basic physical structures (buildings, roads, railroads) needed for the operation of a society.

interned—To take prisoner or to hold captive.

isolationists—People who wanted to stay out of World War II and keep America safe.

lend-lease—A way for President Roosevelt to get military, food, and medical supplies to England.

listing—Angle of degrees when a ship is leaning to one side.

Luftwaffe—German word for the German air force.

magazine—Place to store ammunition and bombs.

ME-109—German fighter plane.

morale—Mental condition of people.

Norden bombsight—American device for dropping bombs on a target.

Nazi Party—German political party brought to power by Hitler in 1933.

protective alliance—An agreement that if one country was attacked, the others would come to its aid.

propaganda—Widespread dissemination or promotion of particular ideas.

RAF—Royal Air Force.

raze—Destroy or burn down.

reprisal—To get back or get even with someone.

stalemate—Situation in which further action is impossible or useless; deadlock.

Stukus—German dive bombers.

Spitfire—British top-of-the-line fighter.

SS—Schutzstaffel, an elite German army unit.

swastika—Ancient religious emblem that stood for fertility and good fortune, in the shape of a hooked cross. The Nazis made it a symbol of Aryan supremacy.

US—United States of America.

Bibliography

Listed below are just some of the books I used over the years to compile this book.

Glines, Carroll V. *The Doolittle Raid; America's daring first strike against Japan.* Atglen: Schisser, 1991.

Doolittle, Gen. James Harold. *I Could Never Be So Lucky Again.* New York: Bantam Books, 2001.

Willmott, H. P. *Pearl Harbor.* New York: Sterling, 2001.

Mosley, Leonard. *Backs to the Wall: The Heroic Story of the People of London during World War II.* New York: Random House, 1971.

Lanning, Lt. Col. Michael Lee. *The Battle 100.* Naperville: Sourcebooks, 2000.

Bard, Mitchell G. PhD, *Complete Idiot's Guide to World War ll.* New York: Alpha Books, 2010.

Grant, R. G. *1001 Battles that Changed the Course of World History.* New York: Universe, 2011.

Collier, Richard. *Eagle Day: The Battle of Britain.* New Jersey: Castle Books, 2003.

Ambrose, Stephen E. *Citizen Soldiers*. New York: Touchstone, 1994.

———. *D-Day June 6, 1944*. New York: Touchstone, 1994.

Lord, Walter. *The Miracle of Dunkirk*. New York: Viking Press, 1982.

Murray, Williamson, and Allan R. Millett. *A War to Be Won: Fighting the Second World War*. Cambridge: Harvard College, 2000.

If you would like to order additional copies
of this book, you may order from:

Red Swan Books
PO Box 67063
Lincoln, NE 68506
redswanbooks@gmail.com
www.redswanbooks.com

You have read in this book about how God helped the Allied Forces in World War II. If you would like to know more about how God can help you personally, please contact any of the following organizations.

It is Written
PO Box 6
Chattanooga, TN 37401-9976
www.itiswritten.com
Phone: (888) 664-5573

Amazing Facts
PO Box 1058
Roseville, CA 95678-8058
www.amazingfacts.org
Phone: (800) 598-7275

Amazing Facts Ministries (Canada)
PO Box 449
Creston, BC V0B 1G0
www.amazingfacts.org
Phone: (250) 402-6070
Toll-Free #: 1 (888) 402-6070

Three Angels Broadcasting Network (3ABN)
PO Box 220
West Frankfort, IL 62896
www.3abn.org
Phone: (618) 627-4651

Notes: